Robert Penn Warren's
*All the King's Men*

ROBERT PENN WARREN'S

# *All the King's Men*

## A READER'S COMPANION

JONATHAN S. CULLICK

UNIVERSITY PRESS OF KENTUCKY

Copyright © 2018 by The University Press of Kentucky

Scholarly publisher for the Commonwealth,
serving Bellarmine University, Berea College, Centre College of
Kentucky, Eastern Kentucky University, The Filson Historical Society,
Georgetown College, Kentucky Historical Society, Kentucky State
University, Morehead State University, Murray State University,
Northern Kentucky University, Transylvania University, University of
Kentucky, University of Louisville, and Western Kentucky University.
All rights reserved.

*Editorial and Sales Offices:* The University Press of Kentucky
663 South Limestone Street, Lexington, Kentucky 40508-4008
www.kentuckypress.com

Library of Congress Cataloging-in-Publication Data

Names: Cullick, Jonathan S., author.
Title: Robert Penn Warren's All the King's Men : a reader's companion /
    Jonathan S. Cullick.
Description: Lexington : University Press of Kentucky, 2018. | Includes
    bibliographical references and index.
Identifiers: LCCN 2018012000| ISBN 9780813175928 (hardcover : acid-
free paper) | ISBN 9780813175942 (pdf) | ISBN 9780813175935 (epub)
Subjects: LCSH: Warren, Robert Penn, 1905-1989. All the king's men.
Classification: LCC PS3545.A748 A793 2018 | DDC 813/.52—dc23
LC record available at https://lccn.loc.gov/2018012000

This book is printed on acid-free paper meeting
the requirements of the American National Standard
for Permanence in Paper for Printed Library Materials.

Manufactured in the United States of America

Member of the Association of University Presses

For Cheryl

He could t-t-talk so good. The B-B-Boss could. Couldn't nobody t-t-talk like him.

—Robert Penn Warren, All the King's Men

# Contents

# Preface

Late in the summer of 2017, during the first week of school, my Facebook feed was filled with first-day photographs of children entering kindergarten, senior year of high school, and all grades in between. As I scrolled through my iPhone screen, I surveyed pictures posted by the parents of those eager boys and girls with bright backpacks and squeaky new shoes, all calling for plenty of like-button clicks. These images warmed my teacher heart. As a citizen, I took comfort in the uplifting photos. They provided a counterweight to the relentless, depressing, frustrating items passing across the news feed. This was the week when Charlottesville, Virginia, exploded in violence as neo-Nazis, Ku Klux Klan members, and other white supremacists marched in protest against the removal of a statue of Confederate general Robert E. Lee. They brandished signs and yelled slogans of hate against Jews, minorities, and immigrants. They shouted the Nazi slogan "Blood and soil!," a message repugnant to the ideals of a pluralistic nation—a nation founded not upon race but upon its citizens' assent to the self-evident proposition that all human beings are created equal and endowed with the inalienable rights of life, liberty, and happiness. Opponents protested against the "alt-right" marchers, and one of the counterprotestors, a young woman, was killed when (as alleged at the time of this writing) a white supremacist drove his car deliberately into the group. Two police officers on airborne patrol were killed when their helicopter crashed.

Some of our nation's leaders—Virginia's governor, US senators, former presidents—spoke to the nation in their attempts to settle the situation and quench the flames. Others chose to fan the fire. This was the choice of our elected officials in government: to calm the crowds or to rouse them, to be the quiet center of the storm or to be the storm itself. They enacted their choices through the rhetoric of their statements and words, their gestures and tones, their decisions to speak or be silent.

*All the King's Men* is well regarded for being a political story. Based on the life of Louisiana governor Huey Long, it presents the career of a populist demagogue. Reaching back to the Civil War and taking the reader up to the brink of World War II, it is a novel about history and our use of the past. Fundamentally, though, the novel is about language. Politics is conducted through language. Demagoguery is a style of language. Populism is as much a manner of speaking as it is a political program. The novel intrigues us with its evolution of a politician who could not reach people through their intellects but learned how to move them by touching their beliefs, values, prejudices, and resentments. Charting the rise of an authoritarian figure such as the fictional Willie Stark or the all too real Huey Long, Benito Mussolini, Adolf Hitler, or George Wallace means analyzing his use of language. *All the King's Men* troubles us because it forces us to realize that the list of those popular speakers I just named keeps growing. Robert Penn Warren called his novel an "old drama of power and ethics." It is a new drama, too.

That is what stirs the discomfort of the reader ready to relax with Warren's novel and perhaps a cup of coffee, discovering that the narrative hits close to home, discloses something that cannot be ignored. "I know a politician like this," the reader realizes. Maybe even "I voted for someone like this." Who is that politician? Different readers will fill in the blank with different names. Not only is the drama old, but it also travels easily and can speak many languages.

It is portable enough to be carried to any town or county or state capital in the United States. It can travel to another country. It can travel to Washington, DC. A man (it's usually a man) who craves power, who develops the charisma to draw people to himself, and who develops the skill with language to seduce them—that story does not have a boundary. The story of "we the people" who lack something that he and only he can supply—we who have something within ourselves that feels so wounded that only he can heal it—is a story unlimited by any place or time.

This is why we must read and re-read and continue to talk about *All the King's Men*.

*All the King's Men* is one of the great political novels in US literature. It was a best seller, won the Pulitzer Prize, and became an Academy Award–winning movie. Depicting the rise and fall of a dictatorial southern politician, the timeless story with memorable characters raises questions about the importance of history, moral conflicts in public policy, and idealism in government.

This book that you are holding was conceived at the intersection of several interests and projects. The seventieth anniversary of any celebrated novel is an occasion for revisiting an author's work, but for the political novel *All the King's Man* the anniversary year 2016 coincided with major national changes, global changes, and new anxieties. The time was right for revisiting the classic story of Willie Stark.

Accordingly, the Kentucky Humanities Council launched into the planning of a year-long "Kentucky Reads" program for 2018–2019, selecting *All the King's Men* to be the featured novel. The year-long celebration and statewide discussion of the novel coincide with the release of a public-television documentary on the life and work of Robert Penn Warren. This book is intended to serve as a reader's companion for the Kentucky Humanities Council program in partnership with the University Press of Kentucky.

The immediate question animating this study was: How is *All the King's Men* relevant in our time, decades after its publication? To answer that question, it seemed appropriate to interview a cross section of elected and appointed officials as well as journalists in Kentucky to find out how the novel has influenced the work they do or the way they reflect on their work. I sent out more than seventy invitations to individuals in all three branches of Kentucky government and in balanced numbers across the political aisle, including officeholders at the highest levels, as well as to journalists and university presidents. I asked them if they would be able to provide a few sentences expressing their thoughts about the novel. Specifically, my questions were:

1. When and why did you read *All the King's Men?* Was it an assignment in high school or college? Did you read it on your own?
2. What are your general thoughts about *All the King's Men?* Is your impression of the novel favorable or unfavorable?
3. How do you think *All the King's Men* is relevant to Kentucky and our nation today? Do you think there are lessons that government officials or citizens could learn from *All the King's Men?*

Admittedly, my invitation put the recipients on the spot. What if someone had not read the novel in a long time or at all and didn't have time to re-read it or to read it for the first time? The novel is lengthy and intense, and unless a recipient of my request was immediately familiar with it, that request was an imposition. I received a heartening number of answers to my queries, however, indicating an interest in contributing responses. Ultimately, thirteen individuals sent me full responses to my questions, for which I am grateful.

Their responses illuminate concerns about the responsible use of power in the second decade of twenty-first-century America. A few individuals always desire power, and many more are repeatedly drawn like magnets to the energy of power. This is a characteristic of human nature that remains the same even as new modes of communication emerge. Demagoguery has a new technological toolbox, and as soon as we figure out how to use one tool, another emerges. The technologies of the demagogue outrun our ability to grasp the effects they have on us before it is too late.

But, ironically, the constancy of human nature does offer stability. We can't be surprised when we know what to expect. Regardless of the mode of communication, we can figure out what the tyrants and dictators are doing even before they do it. Willie Stark, we are told, "could talk so good." "Sure," the sardonic Jack Burden replies, "he was a great talker." Jack is onto something; he knows what Willie is up to. He even coaches Willie to stop giving speeches that appeal to the intellect and just go for the gut. Dumb it down. "For Sweet Jesus' sake," he says, "don't try to improve their minds."[1] That advice might be cynical, but perhaps it works for the better because sometimes it seems that every purported voter education program is nothing more than another partisan attempt at manipulation—pandering and push polls, wedge issues and dog whistles. Citizens must learn how this kind of rhetoric works. We must be able to identify how language is weaponized. We must be able to name and recognize the strategies of persuasion. No politician is going to do that for us (not even the most well intentioned, and, call me naive, but I do believe the well-intentioned ones are the majority). The implication of Jack's advice is simple: we must improve our own minds. Or perhaps Willie Stark is improving us anyway, despite himself. *All the King's Men* is, among many other things, an instructive book. It depicts the politically motivated manipulation of language in all its manifestations of crudeness and refinement. If effective rhetoric is saying the right thing at the right time, then Robert Penn Warren nailed it. This novel is the textbook for our time.

*Introduction*

# "Tell Me a Story"

If you drive to the small town of Guthrie, located in Todd County, southern Kentucky, you will be greeted by a sign proudly announcing that you are entering the birthplace of the nation's first poet laureate and three-time Pulitzer Prize recipient, Robert Penn Warren. When I was a graduate student at the University of Kentucky in the 1990s, working on my dissertation on Warren, my wife, Cheryl, and I made this trip a couple of times. Drive to the corner of Third and Cherry Streets, and you will arrive at a charming red house, the Birthplace Museum. An official Commonwealth of Kentucky historical marker (marker no. 1879) introduces the house.

> A native of Guthrie, Warren was one of nation's most prolific writers, a world-renowned man of letters. Graduate of Vanderbilt Univ., summa cum laude, 1925; member of the Fugitives (writers group). Rhodes scholar at Oxford, 1928–1930; and twice a Guggenheim Fellow. He was professor of English at La. State, Minnesota, and Yale universities.

And on the reverse side of the marker:

Robert Penn Warren, 1905–1989 Designated "First Poet
Laureate of the United States" by Congress on February 26,
1986. To date only person to receive a Pulitzer Prize in both
fiction and poetry. Warren was a three-time winner of the
Pulitzer Prize: 1947 in fiction for *All the King's Men;* 1958 in
poetry for *Promises;* 1979 in poetry for *Now and Then: Poems
1976–1978.*

Every year on or around April 24, writers and their readers
throughout the state of Kentucky convene in the capitol building
in Frankfort to observe Kentucky Writers' Day, a day of celebration sponsored by the Kentucky Arts Council to honor the commonwealth's former and current poets laurate. Visitors can meet the
authors who inspire them and hear the authors give readings of their
works, and every other year the celebration features a special ceremony to induct the state's new poet laureate. The date April 24 was
not chosen arbitrarily; on the contrary, it was a deliberate decision: it
is the birthday of Robert Penn Warren.[1]

The annual celebration in April 2005 was augmented by
another special event hosted in Warren's hometown. The City of
Guthrie held a week-long celebration of the one hundredth anniversary of Warren's birth, which culminated in a ceremony on April
22 to dedicate a US postage stamp being issued to honor Warren
and his work. Cheryl and I had the pleasure of attending this day of
festivities. The town's mayor and members of Warren's family were
in attendance, as were many of the town's citizens and visitors who
made the trip for the day (including scholars and educators participating in the Robert Penn Warren Circle conference at Western Kentucky University in Bowling Green). First-day releases of the
stamp and commemorative items could be purchased, courtesy of
the US Post Office in Guthrie. Ann Wright, Kentucky's US Postal
Service district manager, said, "It is an honor to celebrate the life

and accomplishments of Robert Penn Warren. . . . His powerful ability as a poet and author—as three Pulitzer Prizes attest—is unmatched." The festive atmosphere of the day—with food, activities for children, tours of the Warren museum, and participation of local businesses and civic organizations—made it clear that Guthrie is proud of its native son.[2]

That native son left Kentucky to attend Vanderbilt University at the age of sixteen (in 1921), then the University of California at the age of twenty (in 1925), and finally Yale University at twenty-two (in 1927). In 1931, he would be named acting assistant professor at Vanderbilt, and in 1934 he would be appointed assistant professor at Louisiana State University. Subsequent travels and career moves would take him to Italy, Iowa, Minnesota, New York, France, and Vermont, among other locations far from home. Yet he returned to Kentucky throughout his life, sometimes physically to visit family, but more often he visited imaginatively to reconnect with the people and places that would supply him with material for writing.

From 1958 to 1963, Warren wrote narrative essays that were printed as articles in *Holiday* magazine. These historical narratives incorporated elements of the personal travelogue. Some were about Texas history, but one of them brought him back to Kentucky. "The World of Daniel Boone" is a travel piece that takes you, the reader, on a trip to Boonesborough, Kentucky: "On U.S. 60, east out of Lexington, that is probably the way you will go—out past the great horse farms of Kentucky, the hunt club and the swelling pastures and white paddocks and stone walls and noble groves. It is beautiful country, even now. It was once thought to be Eden."

Your road trip proceeds until you arrive at Pilot Knob and a retelling of the story of Boone's entry into in Kentucky.

The date: October 10, 1773. Sixteen-year-old James Boone, the eldest son of Daniel Boone, has been injured and captured.

Impatient with local Indians' reluctance to sell their land rights in Kentucky, Daniel Boone had led a group, including James, from Tennessee through the mountain trace. On that fall night, a small group of stragglers that had ventured about three miles from the main camp was attacked. For the rest of that harrowing night, James was tortured to death. When the bodies were discovered, "there was little leisure for mourning" as Boone's party immediately prepared to counterattack. Ultimately, this event prompted the would-be settlers to delay their plans.

In the aftermath, Boone and his family stayed in Kentucky for the winter, but in late spring the father "made a solitary pilgrimage" to the grave of his fallen son. "We can look back on this moment of lonely mourning," Warren tells us, "the most melancholy moment of Boone's life, by his own account—and see it as a moment that gives inwardness and humanity to an age. Beyond the clichés of romance of the frontier, beyond the epic record of endurance and the manipulations of land speculators and politicians, beyond the learned discussions of historical forces, there is the image of a father staring down at the patch of earth."

As readers, we empathize with the parent who looks upon the grave of the child. We share the father's sense of devastating loss, bewildered in his disbelief that the natural order of time has been so violated by his son's death. The moment takes on archetypal significance as Boone becomes every father, and the weight of the sorrow is so monumental that the writer is compelled to render it in the terms of epic. "It is like that moment in the midst of the heroic hurly-burly of the *Iliad* when Hector seeks out his wife and little son, and the baby cries in terror at the great crest of horsehair on the bronze helmet, and Hector lifts off the helmet, lays 'it shining on the ground' and takes his son in his arm."[3]

This brief excerpt illustrates that "the historical sense and the poetic sense should not, in the end, be contradictory," as Warren states in the preface to his book-length poem *Brother to Dragons*.[4]

Returning to historical places and events in person sharpens our perception of the historical experience. We must know the facts of what happened. Making those return trips in the imagination enlivens our sense of the spirit of that historical experience. We must grasp for some truth of what happened.

Literature makes that kind of return possible. Warren connects Boone's moment at the grave to a moment in a great canonical work of literature, Homer's epic of the Trojan War. It is a connection that everyone can understand, many readers having encountered the *Iliad* and the *Odyssey* in high school. With all the connectivity of the twenty-first century—texting and Facetime, Facebook, Twitter, Instagram, and Tumblr—we still connect to history and each other in this elemental way—through the telling and retelling of our stories. The human being, as described by Jonathan Gottschall, is *"the storytelling animal."* Reading, viewing, and listening to stories does not serve merely our entertainment preferences. Narrative is crucial for our survival. Our stories "make us human."[5] We connect to the stories we have read because we seek to be consoled, reassured, and inspired and because our ideas, our beliefs, our values, and even our very identities need to be challenged, confronted, and questioned. With those objectives in mind, I propose that Robert Penn Warren's masterpiece novel *All the King's Men* is more compelling and possibly even more relevant now than ever. It is time for us to return to one of the finest writers in the United States and one of the quintessential works of political fiction in American literature.

Politics is the arena where stories—usually dramas, sometimes tragedies, and occasionally comedies—are played out on a grand stage of human complexities and flaws. These days that stage is built from cable television and the Internet, where reporters, talk-show hosts, bloggers, and pundits provide commentary like a twenty-four/seven Greek chorus. Though I have not done any study of the matter, I would speculate that Shakespeare probably tops the list of writers most often referred to in political commentary. References to plays such as *Julius Caesar, Richard III, Macbeth, Hamlet,* and *Coriolanus* appear occasionally in newspaper opinion pieces. Articles in the *American Spectator* and the *Guardian,* for example, called Hillary Clinton "the Lady Macbeth of Little Rock" and referred to President Barack Obama as "Hamlet on the Potomac."[6] Shakespeare's fictional kings and princes must be some of the most influential leaders in history if measured by the power they exert on our understanding of current events. By that same standard, one of the most influential governors in US history might very well be a work of fiction: Willie Stark of *All the King's Men.* When National Public Radio broadcast what it called a "profile of one of America's greatest and most controversial politicians . . . the quintessential American demagogue," it said of Willie Stark that he was "a champion of the little guy who became a governor and a tyrant" and then it concluded, almost as a quip, "He's also fictional."[7]

Stark is indeed a demagogue who begins with ideals but ends up compromising those high values. In the name of getting good things done, he cuts ethical corners. Warren's novel raises uncomfortable but crucial questions about desired ends and the means used to achieve them. It raises uncomfortable questions about the wielding of power and the role of ethics in politics. It asks us to consider: *How can we enable the coexistence of our values, which we never want to compromise, and our political processes, which demand compromise?* It asks us to consider not only the obligations of our elected leaders but also our own responsibilities as the citizens who give them power. It even asks us to confront the relationship between news reporters and the elected officials they cover.

These questions are pressing upon us at this moment in Kentucky and in the United States. The political landscape of our nation is polarized, with citizens divided into camps that barely speak to each other and fail to acknowledge good faith in each other's positions. Making this polarization worse, unfortunately, too many elected officials, for their own political advantages, are exploiting and even amplifying those rifts rather than attempting to mediate them. Indeed, different sides of arguments even adopt their own sources of news and facts. Here in Kentucky and across our great country, we must dedicate ourselves to finding common ground because in a pluralistic society we have no other option if we aspire to be peaceful and productive. The novel *All the King's Men* provides us one tool for engaging in that civil dialogue. We must return to Warren's story of power and demagoguery, of authoritarianism and corruption, which was prescient when Warren wrote it in the aftermath of the world at war and remains prescient for our contemporary circumstances and all time. As Warren worked on *All the King's Men*, humanity was engaged in the most massive war and slaughter of innocents in the history of the world. Two decades later, as Warren was working on his poem *Audubon: A Vision*, the United States was in conflict with itself, as was very evident in the war in Vietnam, the assassinations of Martin Luther King Jr. and Robert Kennedy, and protests erupting throughout the nation. Warren wrote,

> Tell me a story.
> In this century, and moment, of mania,
> Tell me a story.[8]

We are close to entering the third decade of another century. But literature is timeless, and *All the King's Men* might be more relevant than ever. Let's tell the story.

*1*

# The Life of Robert Penn Warren

## "Do You Still Consider Yourself a Southern Writer?"

The author of *All the King's Men* was born in 1905, the son of Robert Franklin Warren, a small-business proprietor and banker, and Anna Ruth Penn Warren, a schoolteacher. A smart child who loved books, "Rob Penn" attended school with students in upper grades beyond his years. His best friend was one of those older kids, Kent Greenfield, an outstanding baseball player who would go on to a brief career in the Major Leagues. Young Warren wanted to enter the navy after high school and succeeded with acceptance to the US Naval Academy, but in the spring of 1921 he suffered an injury to his left eye from a rock-throwing incident with his younger brother. The injury eventually led to removal of the eye and cancellation of his appointment to the academy. This tragic turn of fortune steered the teenager into a life-changing direction that would eventually alter the course of poetry, fiction, and literary studies in America. In the fall of 1921, he entered Vanderbilt University at the age of sixteen. There he met teachers in English who were among the literary giants of their time: Allen Tate, John Crowe Ransom, and Andrew Lytle. His professors quickly recognized their student's talents as a writer, particularly in poetry, and invited him to join them in a group that would become known as the Fugitives, publishing their own journal of poetry. Later, many of this group would reconfigure themselves as the Agrarians, with the young Warren a contributor to their volume of essays *I'll Take My Stand* (1930).

In 1925, Warren graduated from Vanderbilt summa cum laude and entered the University of California at Berkeley as a graduate student and teaching assistant. Here he met his first wife, Emma "Cinina" Brescia. In 1927, he received his MA from the University of California and in the fall entered Yale University on fellowship. In October 1928, he entered New College at Oxford as a Rhodes scholar and received his BLitt in the spring of 1930. He married Emma Brescia in the summer of 1929, a marriage that was to end in 1951. In 1952, he married Eleanor Clark. They had two children, Rosanna Phelps Warren and Gabriel Penn Warren.

Warren was a poet, critic, novelist, and teacher. He taught at Vanderbilt University (Nashville, Tennessee), Southwestern College (Memphis, Tennessee), University of Minnesota (Minneapolis), Yale University (New Haven, Connecticut), and Louisiana State University (Baton Rouge). While at LSU, he founded and edited, along with Cleanth Brooks and Charles W. Pipkin, the literary quarterly the *Southern Review.*

He was appointed poet laureate of the United States in 1986—the nation's first poet laureate upon the creation of that position. He published sixteen volumes of poetry, two of which, *Promises: Poems, 1954–1956* (1957) and *Now and Then: Poems, 1976–1978* (1978), received Pulitzer Prizes. Warren published ten novels. *All the King's Men* was awarded the Pulitzer Prize, and the movie made of it with Broderick Crawford and Mercedes McCambridge in 1949 won Academy Awards for Best Motion Picture, Best Actor, and Best Supporting Actress. In addition, he published a book of short stories, a biography, critical essays, three historical essays, critical studies of American writers (Herman Melville, Theodore Dreiser, John Greenleaf Whittier), and two studies of race relations in America. As of this writing, he is the only author to have received Pulitzer Prizes in two genres—fiction and poetry. Other honors include the Bollingen Prize, the National Medal for Literature, and the Presidential Medal of Freedom.

Warren collaborated with his LSU colleague Cleanth Brooks in writing several textbooks in the teaching of literature (*An Approach to Literature* [1936], *Understanding Poetry* [1938], *Understanding Fiction* [1943], and *American Literature: The Makers and the Making*, 2 vols. [1973]) and composition (*Modern Rhetoric* [1949]). The publication of *Understanding Poetry* established his reputation as one of the leading representatives of the movement in literary criticism called New Criticism, which focused readers and students on how the elements and techniques of a literary text work together to create meanings, ironies, and ambiguities, all of which form a unified work. These "new critical" textbooks helped revolutionize the teaching of literature in university and high school classrooms throughout the nation.

From the 1950s until his death in 1989, Warren lived in Connecticut and at his summer home in Vermont. He is buried at Stratton, Vermont. A memorial marker is situated in the Warren family gravesite in Guthrie, Kentucky.[1]

*"Do you still consider yourself a Southern writer, even though you have been away so long?"* This question was posed to Robert Penn Warren in an interview in 1977 by Peter Stitt, the professor from my undergraduate days who introduced me to Warren's work when he assigned our American literature class some poems from Warren's Pulitzer Prize–winning collection *Now and Then*. The inter-

view took place in Warren's home in Fairfield, Connecticut. The writer's response: "I can't be anything else. You are what you are. I was born and grew up in Kentucky, and I think your early images survive. Images mean a lot of things besides pictures."[2] Years earlier, Warren had referred to himself as a "displaced person" from the American South, saying that it had been "a long time, but I don't get entirely used to it."[3] The short answer to Professor Stitt's question is clearly *yes*.

Warren returned to Kentucky imaginatively for many of the settings, stories, and images in his creative work. His first published novel, *Night Rider* (1939), is set in the tobacco war of 1905–1908 between independent tobacco growers in Kentucky and large tobacco companies. Chapter 4 of *All the King's Men* (1946) includes an interpolated story set in Kentucky featuring the journals of Cass Mastern, a forebear of the narrator, Jack Burden. Mastern had an affair with his friend's wife, was unable to rescue an enslaved woman who had suffered as a result of his wrongdoing, and consequently sent himself off to the Civil War for expiation of his sin. *World Enough and Time* (1950) is the fictionalized version of an event in 1826 known as the "Kentucky Tragedy," in which Jereboam Beauchamp killed Colonel Solomon Sharp, a rising star in Kentucky politics, for the alleged seduction of Beauchamp's wife, Ann Cook. Beauchamp was convinced that Sharp, to advance his own political reputation, had published a broadside accusing Ann of becoming pregnant by a slave. Ann lived with Jereboam in his prison cell as he awaited execution, ultimately attempting suicide with him. She died, but he was given treatment that allowed him to live long enough to be hanged. At their request, they were interred together within the same grave in a Nelson County, Kentucky, cemetery.

Warren's book-length poem *Brother to Dragons* (1953) recalls the murder of a slave in 1811 by a nephew of Thomas Jefferson in Smithland, Kentucky, which is located in Livingston County near

Paducah. *Band of Angels* (1955) is about Amantha Starr, a girl raised in Kentucky before the Civil War. Upon her father's death, it is learned that she is legally considered black and is thus sold into slavery. *The Cave* (1959) is based on an incident that became a national news sensation of a boy who was trapped in a Kentucky cave. *Jefferson Davis Gets His Citizenship Back* (1980) concerns the Confederate president, who was born and attended college in Kentucky, and the monument that was erected in his honor in Todd County. *Portrait of a Father* (1988) is Warren's memoir of Robert Franklin Warren. More of his works found their settings or inspirations in Kentucky, including a number of his poems. Some of his late poems, included in *Now and Then: Poems 1976–1978,* feature his memories of himself as a boy exploring and growing up in his Kentucky hometown. Similarly, his poem *Audubon: A Vision* (1969) concludes with Warren returning to his home state in his memory:

> Long ago, in Kentucky, I, a boy, stood
> By a dirt road, in first dark, and heard
> The great geese hoot northward.[4]

# 2

# An Overview of
# *All the King's Men*

## "The Awful Responsibility of Time"

Readers of *All the King's Men* might get a chuckle from hearing that Robert Penn Warren predicted that it would be "rather a shortish" book. As the author commenced drafting the manuscript of the novel in 1943, he wrote to his editor, Lambert Davis, "I don't see it as a very long book." One year later he wrote a more realistic assessment to Allen Tate: "I had hoped to make it a fairly compact book, but it now looks like a long, long son-of-a-bitch. I've finished about 80,000 words and haven't neared the halfway mark. God help me."[1] We readers are the beneficiaries of Warren's original miscalculation, for had he been economical with his words, we would not have the multilayers and counterpoints of time periods, memories, plot lines, character relationships, themes, and conflicts that the complete novel gives us. Depending on the edition, the published novel can total five hundred to six hundred or more pages. The synopsis in this chapter, in contrast, is truly very "shortish"—such a quick overview that it does not even scratch the surface. I mention its brevity simply to affirm the obvious point that the best and only way to appreciate the richness and intensity of such a great work of fiction is, of course, to read it. With that important caveat in mind, I offer a synopsis here to initiate the novel's new reader and provide a review for the veteran. Spoiler alert.

The setting of *All the King's Men* is an unnamed southern state. But the novel seems set in Louisiana, not only because of the Huey Long connection but also because of occasional references to cotton fields, pine woods in the northern part of the state, and a large body of water on the coast. The novel's plot is complex, with many characters and subplots, but here is the general story minus some subplots.

The year is 1939. Jack Burden, a former newspaper reporter and now an aide to Governor Willie Stark, narrates the entire novel as a flashback. The novel begins in a car in 1936 as Governor Stark and his staff ride out to what we would call a "photo op" at Stark's home with his wife, Lucy; his son, Tom; and his father. The car is driven by Sugar-Boy, Stark's driver and bodyguard, who carries a .38-caliber revolver. Also in the group is Sadie Burke, Stark's politically savvy assistant with whom he later has an affair. Jack recalls meeting Stark in 1922, back when Willie seemed awkward and naive, but Jack remembers Willie winking at him, foretelling things to come.

While on location during the photo op, Stark learns that Judge Irwin, a good friend of Jack and his mother, is supporting an opposing candidate, Callahan, who is backed by Stark's opponent, Mac-Murfee, so they pay a late-night visit to the judge to try to intimidate him to change his endorsement. When Stark's plan to pressure the judge fails, Stark orders Jack to dig up some dirt on the judge to extort his endorsement. In a well-known passage, Stark explains his philosophy of using negative information—dirt—to force positive results. Like God using dirt to create Adam, human beings can use dirt to accomplish their own purposes. When Jack at first tells Stark that the judge is clean—dirt free—Stark evokes Psalm 51 ("I was born guilty, a sinner when my mother conceived me"[2]) and repeats his philosophy that there is dirt everywhere and on everyone. This begins a "historical excursion," as Jack sardonically calls it, a journey into opposition research, though Jack embarks on the project with the intention and expectation of proving that the judge is indeed upright and without corruption.

Jack recalls how Stark rose to power: Willie Stark was originally ineffectual but ambitious. As the county treasurer, he had publicly opposed those political insiders who would arrange the substandard construction of a school building for their own financial gain. A tragedy at the school, the collapse of a fire escape and the deaths and injuries of several children, result in Stark's rise in public stature. When he discovers that he was drafted as a gubernatorial candidate by some political operatives to split the vote for their rival, he throws aside his prepared speech, makes a fiery populist declaration against those who exploited him, and drops out of the race. After returning home and practicing law, he eventually runs again for governor and wins the race. He offers Jack a job to work for him personally, not the state, with the troubling, too vague job description of doing whatever might come up.

Stark's administration is characterized by graft, corruption, intimidation, patronage, and adultery. His justification is that sometimes some grease is needed to make the wheels of government turn. When an underling in the state auditor's office, Byram White, is discovered embezzling government funds, Stark covers up White's involvement in the crime but then forces White to write an undated resignation letter (which Stark will keep at his own discretion until he needs it). Stark later successfully challenges an impeachment attempt because of the White episode and, rather than fire White, resists the charges in order to avoid giving his opponents any victory. On principle, Stark's attorney general, Hugh Miller, resigns.

In an effort to create something free from any taint—something truly clean and dirt free—Stark decides to build a hospital for the poor people in his state. To give the hospital respectability, Stark wants Adam Stanton to be its director. Adam and his sister, Anne, are childhood friends of Jack. Adam and Jack have been close for many years, and Anne has been the object of Jack's romantic interests for many years, dating back to when they were teenagers swimming in the idyllic waters of Burden's Landing. Adam is now a highly respected physician, a man of ideals, the son of former governor Joel Stanton. Adam hesitates to accept the offer because of his disagreement with Stark's methods. They meet and discuss their competing moral philosophies. Stark articulates his belief that all humanity is corrupt; therefore, the good can never be created per se but must always be produced out of the bad. He draws an analogy to steam pressure, which if neglected can result in an explosion but if put to productive use can generate a locomotive.

Anne tries to convince Adam to accept the position, and at Stark's direction Jack eventually convinces Adam by showing him the information he has dug up on the judge. Jack's "Case of the Upright Judge" did indeed uncover corruption from the days when Irwin was attorney general—corruption that went all the way up to the then governor, Joel Stanton, Adam and Anne's father.

To build his hospital, Stark adamantly refuses to do any deals with Tiny Duffy and contractor Gummy Larsen, corrupt friends of his opponent, MacMurfee. However, Stark's son, Tom, has impregnated a girl. Those same political opponents use that potential scandal to blackmail Stark into engaging in a construction deal for the hospital. In hopes of coercing Judge Irwin to put pressure on Mac-Murfee, whom the judge has supported, Stark wants whatever information Jack has dug up on the judge. When Jack confronts Irwin with the information he eventually finds, Irwin commits suicide. Jack's mother then reveals that Irwin was his father.

With Irwin dead, Stark must give the hospital contract to Larsen, but when Tom is severely injured in a football accident, Stark withdraws from the deal and pledges to name the hospital after Tom. Adam finds out that Anne has had an affair with Stark— information that Jack, to his shock, had discovered earlier. This affair also explains why Anne persuaded Adam to accept the hospital director job. Adam, the man of ideals who resists corruption, assassinates Stark and is shot to death by Sugar-Boy in the process. Jack is left to piece together the meaning of all that has happened. He reconciles his relationship with his mother and with Anne. He remains in politics, this time deciding to join Hugh Miller, Stark's former attorney general. The year is 1939, and the storms of war have formed over Europe. Jack and Anne are leaving Burden's Landing to go into the world with each other and their new knowledge.

The novel became a widely reviewed best seller immediately upon its publication. Numerous reprints eventually appeared, including translations into more than two dozen languages and recognition with the Pulitzer Prize for Fiction. Most of the initial reviews were positive, Harold Woodell observes in his overview of the novel's reviews, with some reviewers faulting the novel mostly "on polemical grounds—the book had neither roundly denounced totalitarianism nor portrayed the demagogue as a villainous tyrant from first to last." Such criticisms missed the tragic contradictions that Warren was using to depict Stark as an idealist whose goals are corrupted by his methods. But appreciation for the novel's ethical concerns would increase with time. Indeed, "if the initial reception was somewhat mixed, the critical attention *All the King's Men* received grew dramatically over the next few years until the book was universally hailed as one of the great American novels of the twentieth century."[3] Noting that "the most perceptive reviewers saw

*All the King's Men* also as a brilliant novel with philosophical dimensions," Joseph Blotner, Warren's biographer, says that over time the novel has become "one of the most extensively analyzed in modern American literature."[4] The British *Guardian* and the Modern Library have put *All the King's Men* on their lists of "100 best novels."[5]

# *All the King's Men* in Political and Popular Culture

## "This Race Is Starting to Remind Us of a Novel"

Inspired by Huey P. Long, the governor (1928–1932) and US senator (1932–1935) of Louisiana, Willie Stark has been showing up lately in our national conversations. Politicians from all ends of the political spectrum—liberal and conservative, Republican and Democratic—have been compared to Willie "the Boss" Stark. These analogies have been drawn in sufficient number to edify and irritate every American voter regardless of political orientation or party.

Consider a few examples. In 2009–2010, Illinois governor Rod Blagojevich was impeached, removed from office, and convicted on federal charges. Invoking *All the King's Men,* a newspaper columnist observed that "the parallels between Blagojevich and Stark are jaw-dropping." In my own state of Kentucky, articles published in the *Lexington Herald-Leader* and *Frankfort State Journal* described the administration of former Governor Paul Patton as "a burlesque version of Robert Penn Warren's *All the King's Men*," which in turn was described as the "definitive novel of Southern politics gone wrong . . . [involving] a fictional governor who believed he could shape history." On a national scale, a writer for the *Toronto Star* noted that many of President Barack Obama's supporters, who initially voted for "a figure above and beyond politics," have become his critics and "wish Obama had a little more in him of Willie Stark, the ruthlessly effective politician at the centre of the greatest novel ever written about American politics: *All the King's Men*." Such criticism, perhaps, saw Obama's flaw in his being too much a man of ideals (like Adam Stanton) and too little a man of action (like Willie Stark).[1]

The presidential election of 2016 initiated a resurgence of references to *All the King's Men* on a Shakespearean scale. Michael Washburn of WFPL radio called the novel "this election season's essential book," opining about the Hillary Clinton versus Donald Trump matchup: "In our current political season—this long, painful, embarrassing, unproductively polarized deliberation on two of the most unpopular candidates in our history—*All the King's Men* provides both commentary and relief. Commentary because of its subject. Relief because of its sophistication." During the primaries, a *Washington Post* journalist described the Hillary Clinton versus Bernie Sanders struggle as "the fight between an idealist and a pragmatist . . . an old one in politics, captured years ago by Robert Penn Warren in his novel *All the King's Men*." (Incidentally, as that opinion piece notes, in the novel, two such individuals, one who lives by ideas and the other who lives by facts, "'were doomed to destroy each other.'")[2]

Comparisons with President Donald Trump have abounded from both conservative and liberal commentators alike. Jonah Goldberg of the *National Review* observes: "As the fictionalized Huey Long character Willie Stark says in the novel *All the King's Men*: 'Your will is my strength. Your need is my justice.' Long promised to make 'every man a king.' Trump promises to make everyone a winner." Some writers consider the novel to be a dystopian forecast of the future, like George Orwell's novel *1984*. Dwight Garner of the *New York Times* says that, "by wide consensus, it's America's essential political novel" and that "it is also eerily prescient, in its portrait of the rise of a demagogue, about some of the dark uses to which language has been put in this year's election." Terry Teachout of the *Wall Street Journal,* also writing about "the prescience of a political novel," says that *All the King's Men* "is more relevant today than ever before" and "is timely because of the brilliant clarity with which it shows how a shrewd politician can connect with those working-class voters who believe that the existing parties don't care about them and are looking for a strong, fearless leader to watch their backs." Teachout concludes that Warren "looked 70 years into the future and foretold the coming of a populist demagogue who spoke the language of the plain people." Mark Caleb Smith of the *Dayton Daily News* compares Trump's aides to Willie Stark's aides, all of whom he calls the "elite enablers"—those who defend and justify "outlandish statements" and "division."[3] These quotations are only a sampling of the references to Warren's novel in articles and blogs. References too numerous to list here proliferate in scholarly journals and books in the fields of legal studies and political science.

Popular culture and the arts in the United States have featured some highly visible references to *All the King's Men,* the most well-known examples being best-selling books that critique the presidency of Richard Nixon and the campaign methods of Bill Clinton and Hillary Clinton. Warren's novel was clearly the inspiration for the title *All the President's Men,* the book by *Washington Post* reporters Bob Woodward and Carl Bernstein about their investigation of the Watergate break-in and Nixon's administration. As preeminent Warren scholar William Bedford Clark observes, Woodward and Bernstein "could safely assume that the allusion of their title would not be lost." They wrote their account with compelling novelistic energy, telling the story of a politician who used questionable or illegal means to achieve what he thought were justifiable ends. As in Warren's novel, which is narrated by a newspaper reporter turned political aide, Jack Burden, the narrators are journalists doing research. Woodward takes Deep Throat's advice to "follow the money," which is precisely the same investigative method Jack uses to track down the dirt on Judge Irwin. Warren suggested a similarity between the two books when he referred to the Huey Long regime as a "world of pure melodrama. Nothing like it since, well, until Watergate, as far as melodrama's concerned. . . . It was tragedy, too."[4]

The novel *Primary Colors,* published by "Anonymous" but later revealed to have been written by *Newsweek* reporter and columnist Joe Klein, uses character types from *All the King's Men* in a plot that critiques the reelection campaign of President Bill Clinton, including many of his aides and especially Hillary Clinton.[5] Klein even creates character names similar to those in *All the King's Men* in explicit allusions to the earlier novel. The main character, Governor Jack Stanton (a portmanteau of "Jack Burden" and "Adam Stanton" from Warren's novel), is most certainly a representation of Bill Clinton. His charisma and magnetic handshake are similar to Willie Stark's ability to relate to the voters. However, similar to Willie Stark, he also has a dark side, creating his own sexual scandals and employing opposition research to destroy political opponents. *Primary Colors* features an opposition researcher similar to Jack Burden, a woman nicknamed "the Dust Buster," echoing Willie Stark's use of the term *dirt* to describe his strategy of destroying opponents. Like Jack Burden with his philosophical struggles, she struggles with the ethics of using such information and realizes that all human beings are united in common flaws. She argues that one ought to win campaigns by having better ideas. As in Warren's novel, the use of damaging information inflicts destructive consequences that are both unpredicted and unintended.

Given the influence of movies, the film industry has embedded *All the King's Men* more deeply into American popular culture. The film of *All the President's Men* was released by Warner Brothers in 1976. With a screenplay by William Goldman and directed by Alan J. Pakula, it stars Robert Redford and Dustin Hoffman as the two sleuthing reporters (with an all-star cast that includes Jack Warden, Martin Balsam, Hal Holbrook, and Jason Robards). Universal Studios released *Primary Colors,* screenplay by Elaine May and directed by Mike Nichols, in 1998. It stars John Travolta, Emma Thompson, and Billy Bob Thornton, supported by Adrian Lester, Maura Tierney, Paul Guilfoyle, Larry Hagman, and Kathy Bates. Considering the proximity of these movies to the presidential administrations they depicted, audiences could take pleasure in quickly recognizing the characters and situations.

Warren's novel was also produced in film, though with little reference to Huey Long or Louisiana. In 1949, Columbia Pictures released *All the King's Men,* written and directed by Robert Rossen. The film won the Academy Award for Best Picture of the Year. It starred Broderick Crawford in a multilayered portrayal of Willie Stark as a tough guy with personal vulnerabilities (winning him a well-deserved Academy Award for Best Actor), John Ireland as a competent Jack Burden, and an impressively strong Mercedes McCambridge as Sadie Burke (her captivating performance earning her the Academy Award for Best Supporting Actress).

This film, highly successful with the critics and at the box office, did take some major departures from the novel. The setting was placeless, definitely not any southern state and distinguished neither by the name of a locale nor by any easily recognizable accents. In a letter in 1949, Warren himself provided a reason for this choice: "They had to change the locale from the South to a Western state—fear of legal difficulties, etc. And there's one advantage in the fact—they don't fool with phoney [*sic*] Southern accents."[6] The film eliminates the novel's first-person narrative voice of Jack Burden, and John Ireland's performance, in my opinion, makes Jack Burden a little too enthralled with Willie Stark's charisma (in the novel he is not so easily impressed, a characterization that is much more interesting). The Rossen film also removed any attention to Jack Burden's personal story, making it all about Willie Stark. Warren's comments on the movie offer praise along with some critique of its departures from the novel, conflicting feelings he resolved with a sense of pragmatism: "[Rossen] made a damn good movie of it. But about two-thirds through he left my character entirely and made a total villain out of Stark: the fascist brute. My man, you see, gets some redemption out of the novel . . . dies repentant." Warren told Rossen his views, and Rossen then developed several possible endings and asked Warren which one he favored. Warren stated, "I picked one but said none of them represent what I said in the book." Rossen replied, "'Son,' he said to me, 'when you come to Hollywood you've got to learn one thing—there's not going to be anything called irony in the end of an American picture.'" Ultimately, Warren pragmatically concluded, "It's his movie, not mine."[7]

The Columbia Pictures remake in 2006 was received with much less critical and financial success, but it attempted to adhere more closely to the novel. The screenplay, written by director Steven Zaillian, put the story explicitly in Louisiana, with some scenes even filmed at the Louisiana state capitol building (and with a direct visual reference to Huey Long in the assassination scene). The script used the voice-over narration of Jack Burden and multiple flashbacks to the past to capture the novel's layers of time. Much of Jack Burden's story continues to remain off the screen, but the Zaillian version does connect Burden's past and current life more to the Willie Stark plot than did the Rossen version. Some of that connection gets lost when Jack digs dirt on Willie's political opponents (his investigation into Judge Irwin). In the novel, Jack struggles with the question of whether to stop or continue the investigation; his struggle is internal as he pushes and pulls against himself. In contrast, in Zaillian's film that struggle has been externalized into dialogue with Willie, who pushes Jack against Jack's own better judgment. Nevertheless, Zaillian presents *All the King's Men* as not only the story of Willie Stark but also the story of Jack Burden, which is more in alignment with the novel.

Unfortunately, Zaillian's version does not work well. Reviewers panned the script for tedious storylines and excessive exposition. There is some validity to those criticisms. Characters talk a lot about Willie Stark's corruption, for example, but the script does not show much of that corruption. The critics cited the actors' inconsistent accents and uninspiring performances, and to some extent those critiques are also valid. Sean Penn, an otherwise superb actor, is miscast in the role of Willie Stark. In contrast to the more subdued actors around him, Penn persistently waves his arms, gesticulates, and shouts in an exaggerated accent, making him come across more as a caricature than as a bigger-than-life tragic figure. That performance is so exhausting to watch, it is actually a relief when he is off screen. For some critics (but not all), the actors seemed uncomfortable in their roles and uncertain of their accents. Those observations are occasionally valid but also arguable. Jude Law brings interesting interiority to the role of Jack Burden. James Gandolfini conveys an under-the-surface malevolence in his portrayal of the subservient lieutenant governor Tiny Duffy (though a few critics heard too much New Jersey in his "southern good ol' boy"). Anthony Hopkins is steadfast and tragic as Judge Irwin (and hints of his English accent don't distract as much as some reviewers implied). Kate Winslet and Mark Ruffalo play the siblings Anne and Adam Stanton with no particular distinction but sufficiently. For some critics (but not all), Patricia Clarkson as Sadie Burke offers the strongest performance in the cast (and because she is a native of Louisiana, the one with the most convincing accent). Despite some disappointments in execution, the Zaillian version actually does represent Warren's vision more effectively than the Rossen version. Rossen made a better film, but Zaillian made a better story.[8]

*All the King's Men* has even been interpreted for the stage, initially by the author himself. He recrafted *All the King's Men* as a dramatic script in 1947–1948 that was revised and ultimately produced in 1959. Directed by Mark Schoenberg, starring Clifton James as Willie Stark, John Ragin as Jack Burden, and Marian Reardon as Sadie Burke, the play opened at the East 74th Street Theatre in New York City on October 16, 1959. The play "had a highly successful Off-Broadway run during the 1959 season" and was greeted mostly by very positive reviews. Warren's letters from the time period indicate that he was very pleased with all aspects of the production—the director, the actors, the theater facilities, and the newspaper reviews, particularly the review in the *New York Times.* The script continues to be available for licensing from the Samuel French company for professional, amateur, and student productions.[9]

The next stage interpretation, *Willie Stark, the Opera,* with score and libretto by Carlisle Floyd, premiered at the Houston Grand Opera on April 24, 1981. It opened two weeks later at the John F. Kennedy Center for the Performing Arts in Washington, DC, and was broadcast on PBS in September.[10] Directed by Harold Prince, it starred Timothy Nolen as Willie Stark, Alan Kays as Jack Burden, and Jan Curtis as Sadie Burke. The performances were strong, especially that of Nolen, who portrayed Stark as a convincing, even frightening bully but also inwardly struggling with a sense that he has lost his way. He was at his best in the speech scene, when the lights dimmed and he sang a self-reflective aria telling himself to "come home." For the purpose of this staging, major revisions and condensations were made to the plot. Willie Stark is now a single father. The characters Lucy and Tom, his wife and son in the novel, have disappeared and been replaced by a young daughter, also named Lucy, who was paralyzed in the collapse of a schoolhouse, which ironically led to Willie's rise in politics (because he had tried to stop its substandard construction). Judge Irwin is now "Judge Burden," Jack Burden's father, and there is no Adam Stanton. The assassin is Jack (definitely a major departure from the novel!), motivated by Stark's affair with Anne, Jack's fiancée. Other plot elements were changed, and new ones were added to portray Willie's corruption. Audiences of the opera will come away with the sense that they have seen and heard something that is based on Warren's novel but that also stands as a new work apart from it.

Reviews were mixed as critics found the opera more influenced by the traditions of Broadway musical theater than by opera, an opinion no doubt amplified by the fact that its director, Harold Prince, had recently directed two of Broadway's most notable operatic musicals of the late 1970s, *Evita* and *Sweeney Todd*. Specifically, one reviewer noted that the "controversial opera" had received a "severe critical drubbing" due to its similarities to Broadway musicals in composition and staging. Another noted that the opera "is the subject of some bickering among music critics," asking, "Is it opera, or is it closer to Broadway musical theatre?" That review praised the performances as very strong but curiously avoided saying anything about the score other than noting that it is "eclectic." Another reviewer was not so neglectful of the musical score, calling it "remarkably thin" and "choppy and shortwinded, and so incidental to the action that it sounds almost absentminded," consisting of "strident, prosaic recitative that tears at the listener's patience—and, no doubt, sears the vocal cords." Opera goers who might get a chance to see *Willie Stark* but who have a strong preference for melodies they can hum afterward will have their hopes frustrated, though the score does have its moments, especially during Willie's aria in the speech scene and in a delightful duet between a banjo and a harmonica.[11]

*4*

# The Timelessness of
# *All the King's Men*

## "Willie Stark Was Not Huey Long"

If we consider all of these versions of *All the King's Men*—the films
(Robert Rossen's in 1949 and Steven Zaillian's in 2006), the nonfiction book *All the President's Men,* the novel *Primary Colors,* the
play (1959), and the opera (1981)—we could conclude that Warren's novel, as described by William Bedford Clark, "has become a
part of the overall cultural fabric of the United States to an extent
that is rare for any work of fiction, and its appeal has consistently
spanned the chasm between what we used to call 'high' and 'low'
culture." And if we add the comparisons of Willie Stark to various real-life politicians (regardless of whether we agree or disagree
with the selected comparisons), it is clear, according to Kentucky
Supreme Court justice Sara Combs, that *All the King's Men* is "a tale
for all seasons of politics."[1] The timelessness of this tale raises questions for us: *Why is this novel so timeless and significant? And, more*

*pressing, how are the issues that Warren wrote about seventy years ago relevant to Americans today? Can we apply the lessons of Warren's narrative to our current political atmosphere?*

The author himself might resist these questions because they could be said to limit the novel to a particular place and time. In the introduction to the Modern Library Edition, originally published in the *Sewanee Review,* Warren claimed that the book was not a political tract or a "biography of, and apologia for, Senator Long": "Willie Stark was not Huey Long. Willie was only himself."[2] Warren was responding to the popular and critical assumption—immediate upon the book's publication—that the novel was a biographical fiction of Long. This assumption continues today, and for good reason. Clearly, Huey Long was a model for Stark. Warren taught at Louisiana State University during and after some of the Huey Long years, from 1934 to 1942. Similarities between Stark and Long run throughout the text. Their careers take similar shapes. Both begin in humble circumstances but show early ambition: law school in one year, an unsuccessful first attempt to run for governor, programs of social reform and standing up for common people, descent into corruption, impeachment but a victorious emergence through dubious methods, achievement of absolute power in their states, and ultimate assassination by men who happen to be physicians. Their methods are similar. They force employees to write undated letters of resignation to use at their pleasure. They keep little black books and files holding the damaging research that they uncover on their political enemies. Their speeches are similarly full of populist appeals.[3]

Warren discussed the Huey Long connection, as in one letter from 1943 that mentions his need to do some research for the novel: "Recently, in worrying over the novel coming up (which will probably be called *All the King's Men*) . . . I got the idea of appealing to the Rosenwald people [a foundation] for a grant to enable me to get

South for the summer and work the newspaper files and do a little prying around, gossip, and interview, etc. to heat myself up for the final business on the political novel."[4]

Warren conceded in the introduction to the Modern Library Edition, "I do not mean to imply that there was no connection between Governor Stark and Senator Long. Certainly it was the career of Long and the atmosphere of Louisiana that suggested the play that was to become the novel." However, he continued, "But suggestion does not mean identity, and even if I had wanted to make Stark a projection of Long, I should not have known how to go about it. For one reason, simply because I did not, and do not, know what Long was like." Warren stated elsewhere about those years: "If you were living in Louisiana, you knew you were living in history defining itself before your eyes and you knew that you were not see-ing a half-drunk hick buffoon performing an old routine, but wit-nessing a drama which was a version of the world's drama and the drama of history: the old drama of power and ethics."[5]

Warren reiterated this theme often, as in his interview with Frank Gado (who interviewed many well-known writers) in the 1960s, in which he made a distinction between "writing a story about an actual person and using him as a kind of model":

I don't pretend that Willie Stark is Huey Long. I know Stark, but I have no idea what Long was really like. . . . I knew stories about Long, but that's quite different. What happened with the real Long and what his motives were is [*sic*] between him, his God, and his conscience. There's no way in the world for me, or you, to know that. But I know water runs downhill; and if a bomb explodes, I know that someone lit the fuse. Events don't cause themselves. I saw the end products of Long and I know that men's motives and actions are triggered and operate in certain ways.[6]

So, clearly, the novel was inspired by Huey Long, but Warren, with his sights on an objective broader than depicting the life of one politician, wanted to describe the tragedy of all idealistic leaders whose aspirations to greatness are compromised and corrupted by the very power they seek. Though the story takes place in Louisiana, it reaches back to classical Greek and Shakespearean tragedy and stretches forward up to the author's own time, World War II and beyond. As Joyce Carol Oates notes, characters such as "the charismatic Southern politician Willie Stark have acquired the status of American archetypes, larger than the historically precise fictional worlds they inhabit."[7]

This double vision for the novel is why Warren often talked about his main character in seemingly contradictory ways. He did allow, "If I had never gone to live in Louisiana and if Huey Long had not existed, the novel would never have been written. But this is far from saying that my 'state' in *All the King's Men* is Louisiana . . . or that my Willie Stark is the late Senator. What Louisiana and Senator Long gave me was a line of thinking and feeling that did eventuate in the novel." "How directly did I try to transpose into fiction Huey P. Long and the tone of that world [the world of Louisiana]?" Warren asked.[8] The answer is that the novel actually originated years earlier, in the late 1930s, as a verse play titled *Proud Flesh,* written in the style of a Greek tragedy (including choruses of highway patrol officers, football players and cheerleaders, and surgeons) and with the main character a demagogue who bears only slight resemblance to Huey Long. Warren was in Italy as Benito Mussolini was rising to power, and by the time he started reconstructing the play into the novel, he had left Louisiana. As he started writing the story as the verse play in the Italy of the 1930s, he was "concerned more with the myth than with the fact, more with the symbolic than with the actual." When he started writing the novel, he continued, "I was doing so after I had definitely left Louisiana and the world in which the story had its roots. By now the literal, factual world was only a memory, and therefore was ready to be absorbed freely into the act of imagination."[9] The novel is not a fictionalized account of Long's rise and fall; it is about a fact of human nature that is larger than just one man.

Warren was often emphatic about this point. After the novel was published, he began working on the script for a stage version of *All the King's Men*. He wrote an introductory note for the Italian translation of the play that was published in the Italian magazine *Sipario*. What Warren said about the Huey Long connection—and the Mussolini connection—is very well worth reading:

> In the 1930's I lived in Louisiana. Until September 1935, when he was assassinated by a young physician [Dr. Carl Weiss], Huey Long was the scarcely challenged master of the state. In that atmosphere, punctuated by gun fire in the Capitol, the story that was to become *All the King's Men* began to take shape. . . . I began work on it in Louisiana, worked on it in Italy, in an olive grove overlooking Lake Garda, in the summer of 1938, and finished it in the winter of 1939–40, in Rome, to the music of military boot-heels on the cobbles. So the shadow of a European as well as a home-grown American dictatorship lies over the composition.[10]

Ten years later, during a panel discussion at Vanderbilt University, Warren continued to put the story into its greater context: "Huey Long and Julius Caesar both got killed in the capitol, and there you are. It's as simple as that. It's a germ, an anecdote. And teaching Shakespeare in Louisiana in 1935, you couldn't avoid this speculation."[11]

Melissa Block and Ron Elving of National Public Radio summarize the issue succinctly. For Block, Willie Stark certainly "resembles" Huey Long, but at the same time the character's traits cannot be limited to any one particular politician. Elving similarly notes the universality of the narrative as a "classic cautionary tale of power and corruption." He offers an interesting speculation on the film released in 2006 and the opera staged in 1981, discussed in chapter 3: "The author did not live to see the second film, but he would not have liked seeing his story set in Louisiana, nor would he have approved of having Sean Penn sing this song ["Every Man a King"]." Elving's basis for speculating in this manner is a condition that Warren set for his approval of the opera: he gave permission to Carlisle Floyd to compose the opera version of *All the King's Men* on the condition that Floyd not include the song "Every Man a King." If Elving is correct, then we might speculate further that Warren might not have approved of an explicit Huey Long reference in the Zaillian film. Immediately before the assassination scene, Willie Stark takes the elevator to the main floor of the lobby in the state capitol building (where the assassin, Adam Stanton, waits for him). The camera watches the elevator doors close and then, descending with the elevator, ominously passes over an image of Governor Huey P. Long. The shot is so brief, it is easy to miss. Elving concludes, "Willie Stark is no more than a fictional gloss on Huey Long. . . . Willie was not Huey Long, and the novel was not just about politics. . . . [Warren] was more concerned about another authoritarian figure, Benito Mussolini."[12] In this NPR broadcast, David Madden, professor of English at Louisiana State University, tells Block and Elving that "the reason I teach and write about [*All the King's Men*] as a universal book, and try to stay off Huey Long is because I really do believe that it applies to America. Everybody in it, Willie Stark mainly, is representative of facets of the American experience."[13]

Michael Benson, president of Eastern Kentucky University, also identifies the book's universality and timeless messages, which apply to all areas of life that call upon us to make ethical decisions:

A work of literature becomes a classic because of a certain timeliness, an ability to speak on multiple levels to any generation. *All the King's Men,* though written by a native Kentuckian more than seventy years ago, still holds valuable lessons for all Americans today. Warren said he never intended the book to be about politics, and, indeed, its lessons apply to any venue of life. It's important to remember that Willie Stark set out with the noblest of intentions and highest of ideals but became so enamored with power that he began to cynically demonize every enemy, real or perceived, and fooled himself into thinking that the ends always justified the means. *All the King's Men* remains a powerful cautionary tale about what happens when we forsake our passion for the truth and justice and sacrifice our moral values of honesty and decency on the altar of power.[14]

The universalizing quality of literature empowers us to use stories to consider how we must act in the future. Fictional characters and their situations become real for us, and we appeal to them as we contemplate action for the future. Stories serve as anchors for us, and in those anchors we are compelled to find applications for our current cultural moment.[15] So we ask: *In what way can* All the King's Men *be an anchor for us now? What does* All the King's Men *tell us about power and ethics at this particular time in the history of Kentucky and the United States?*

*5*

# Impressions of
# *All the King's Men*

## "A Tale for All Seasons of Politics"

Let's consider how some prominent individuals in Kentucky politics, education, and journalism address the questions asked at the end of chapter 4. Many readers have positive memories of being introduced to the novel and powerful thoughts about its current relevance. Many initially encountered the novel as a school assignment and developed an appreciation for it either at that time or as they returned to it for later, more mature re-readings. I first read it rather late in my reading life, as a graduate student in the historical fiction seminar taught by Professor Steven Weisenburger at the University of Kentucky. I was relieved to be assigned this book because it had always been one that I wanted to read, and now the opportunity had arrived. I had long known—I had long had the sense—that somehow it was an important book that I must discover for myself. I was quickly drawn to its exploration of the ways in which we remember, understand, and write history. Other readers have been introduced to the novel in school, and then further along in adulthood they returned to the book for later re-readings.

Justice Bill Cunningham of the Kentucky Supreme Court recalls that he "first read the book in college in required reading. But [I] read it again much later when I understood and enjoyed it much better. So I would say I read it on my own." Former Northern Kentucky University president Geoffrey Mearns first read the novel when he was in college at Yale; he then introduced his own students to it when he was a new eleventh-grade English teacher in New Jersey. President Michael Benson of Eastern Kentucky University first read it in a high school honors English class but says, "It wasn't until I majored in political science and history in college that I learned much more about Robert Penn Warren and the life and career of Huey Long that I came to appreciate the novel and its many messages and layers." Kentucky State University president Aaron Thompson was introduced to the novel in his senior English class in high school, but "the first time I truly read it was [in] my sophomore English literature class in college." The first reading of *All the King's Men* for Bill Goodman, executive director of the Kentucky Humanities Council, was in his junior year of high school: "I was sent to private school in Georgia to improve my math skills," he remembers, but, "instead of discovering the tools necessary for deciphering algebraic formulas, I found southern literature." He was fortunate to have a teacher who introduced him to William Faulkner, Tennessee Williams, Harper Lee, and Robert Penn Warren. Al Cross, contributing political columnist for the *Louisville Courier-Journal* and director of the Institute for Rural Journalism and Community Issues at the University of Kentucky, says, "I first read *All the King's Men* in a freshman English class at Western Kentucky University and have long had a favorable impression of it as a deep exploration of human nature and the reality that the workings of democracy are determined by human beings, with all their faults."[1]

Other readers have come to the novel independent of any formal school requirement. Former Kentucky governor Steve Beshear recalls, "I read *All the King's Men* for fun in the years after college. Today, after a long career in public service that included two terms as Kentucky's governor—i.e., having lived many of the scenarios, issues, conflicts, and decision making outlined in the book—I appreciate it on a deeper level." Judge Sara Combs of the Kentucky Court of Appeals recalls reading it on her own and on several occasions discussing it with her husband, former governor Bert T. Combs. Tom Eblen, metro/state columnist and former managing editor for the *Lexington Herald-Leader,* first read it when he was a young reporter working with the Associated Press in Nashville. After attending a symposium at Vanderbilt University where Warren and his colleague Cleanth Brooks spoke on a panel, Eblen looked for a copy of the novel. David Hawpe, former editor of the *Louisville Courier-Journal,* recalls that his father had a copy that he read because "even as a youngster I was fascinated with politics." Jamie Lucke, editorial writer for the *Lexington Herald-Leader,* read it "in my early twenties as a very green newspaper reporter fresh out of the University of Kentucky [Journalism] [S]chool."

What is the effect of this novel on a young reader? Mark Neikirk, director of the Scripps-Howard Center for Civic Engagement and former editor of the *Kentucky Post,* offers this memory of the joys of reading it in his youth:

I first read *All the King's Men* when I was a college student— although I did not read it as a class assignment. At the time, I was in one of those book clubs that give you like ten books for a dollar and then charge you an exorbitant amount for postage. Well, I spent my $1 on a set of three Hemingway novels, three

Faulkner novels, and three Warren novels. . . . I was drawn to the fact that Robert Penn Warren was a Kentuckian, and so I began my reading journey. Already headed into journalism (with a history major), I found *All the Kings Men* a perfect book. It was an inside tour of politics, along with a nice coming-of-age romance thing that resonated, too, including the betrayal part—[taken] at an age when one's heart gets broken, and love, like politics, gets a reality check and takes a step back from blind idealism.

What quality immediately strikes us readers upon picking up *All the King's Men* for the first time and makes us want to keep reading? Most likely, it is the style of writing. As a young reader, Geoffrey Mearns was struck by "the power of the words." My experience with the opening of *All the King's Men* was the same. When I read the novel for the first time, I was awed, and that feeling has always returned to me upon successive readings. The iconic first sentences captivate the reader: "To get there you follow Highway 58, going northeast out of the city, and it is a good highway and new. Or was new, that day we went up it. You look up the highway and it is straight for miles, coming at you, with the black line down the center coming at you and at you."[2] Joyce Carol Oates would agree: "The famous, bravura opening of *All the King's Men* has not lost its power. We begin epic-style, *in medias res,* uncertain of our surroundings as of our destination, or who is in our speeding vehicle with us."[3]

Chapter 1 of *All the King's Men* is a masterpiece of technique. Without exaggeration, I would say that it is one of the best first chapters ever written for a novel. Every main character is introduced in an opening narrative that seamlessly weaves together every major plot line and theme of the novel. Everything emerges in this chapter in the counterpoint of an intricately composed fugue. The narrative depicts speed, yet the narrative pace is slow. The characters are in a hurry, but the narrator is not. We are given the image of an automobile barreling down a highway, zooming past southern scenery that is a blur to its passengers but is intensively described for the reader. The driver is the bodyguard, Sugar-Boy, armed with a .38-caliber revolver, who aims the car in a straight line but occasionally veers it slightly—and intentionally—to run over an animal crossing the road. The main passenger is Willie Stark, the governor, the Boss. The self-absorbed, arrogant, oblivious power of that vehicle becomes a metaphor for Willie Stark's ruthless administration and style of political dealing.

As we are considering the opening of the novel, we should pause a moment to address an issue that emerges in the very first paragraph: the presence of racist language in Jack Burden's narration and in some of the dialogue elsewhere in the novel. The author's use of such disturbing language does not reflect his own views or the views of serious readers, scholars, and teachers of the work. In his memoir *Portrait of a Father,* Warren affectionately recalls a lesson from his father. "One of the children (I may have been the child) used at home a word possibly picked up on the school playground: *nigger.* My father very slowly and objectively said: 'That word will never be used in this house.' It never again was."[4] The use of that word in *All the King's Men* reflects only that the novel is in the genre of contemporary realism. Being true to the reality that he represents in fiction, the writer remains true to the language, however distasteful, of the largely racist southerners during the period depicted (and indeed, all too often, in all regions of the country during our own time period as well).

Jamie Lucke recalls the experience of reading the first few pages of the novel: "What stands out in my memory all these decades later is Warren's writing, specifically the descriptions of traveling through the countryside." Tom Eblen also comments on that striking opening scene: *"All the King's Men* is one of my favorite novels, and I have re-read it several times. It always grabs me on page 3, when Warren launches into a vivid, sweeping description of backwoods Louisiana, its history, character, and people." The passage that Eblen is referencing describes a landscape where forests were felled back when the mills were set up and locals and transients eked out a living from the minimal amount the commissaries paid for day labor. As this passage continues, richly describing the story of many southern communities, Warren puts the reader in a landscape exploited for its natural resources by out-of-town interests that use local labor as cheaply as possible and then leave with their profits, while an impoverished population is left with their deforested land. This summary does not begin to do justice to the richness of Warren's prose. "That is a lot of ground to cover in a single, elegant paragraph," Eblen says. "Descriptive prose doesn't get any better than this. . . . There is so much to like about this book: the beautiful writing, the compelling characters, and the deep exploration of universal flaws in American politics and human nature." It is impossible, Eblen thinks (and I agree), to stop reading after Warren's description of the scene. The passage puts the reader squarely into the world of the novel, and the engaged reader feels compelled to continue reading to the end.

Beyond the immediate power of the writing style, readers are struck by the power of the message, that old drama of power, politics, and ethics that Warren talked about. The novel draws us in because it troubles us without hesitation. It confronts us without apology. It thrusts us from the world of the novel into our own world, into our own history. We may try to ignore the novel's ramifications, we may try to tell ourselves that it's just a story, but we cannot because wherever we live and whenever we are living, we read the political dramas in our newspapers and watch them on our televisions—the dramas of power playing out in our nation and in our states and cities and communities. We see all those Willie Starks in our news feeds. We see their enablers, all those Jack Burdens, on the split-screen cable television interviews. The novel does not offer us an escape. If we're looking for a diversion, we'll need a different kind of novel. *All the King's Men* puts us right where we are in our current political environment, and it commands us to do something about that environment.

Warren created a political and personal drama that emerged from his experience in the Louisiana of the 1930s but connects to contemporary political circumstances. Gary Ransdell, president of Western Kentucky University (home of the Robert Penn Warren Collection), makes this connection in his reading of the novel:

> Robert Penn Warren's *All the King's Men* is timeless. Set in the South and written by a son of the South, its themes could have occurred anywhere in America in most any era—and may be just as relevant in today's uncertain political dynamics as it was seventy-one years ago. Today's tweets and texts may have changed the pace of the 1930s and '40s, but the intrigue crosses the generations. Warren had it all in his most acclaimed story—ambition, power, romance, suspense—all of the elements of a good book, then and now. *All the King's Men* is a must read for students, especially those with literary curiosity of a bygone time in the American South. It is particularly important reading for those who might be pondering a career in politics.

David Hawpe offers a similar perspective: "In some ways, and certainly in its setting, this is a narrative unique to the American experience. I think it's also one of the books people should read in order to understand America's political values and civic culture, which lionizes the self-made individual, resists the strictures of government, and celebrates winning as a self-sufficient good. It belongs on a list that begins with *Huckleberry Finn* and includes *Friday Night*

*Lights*. On the other hand, many of its messages are ancient and universal truths. Pride does indeed come before a fall." Aaron Thompson concurs and adds, "Overall, it is a great work of literature that touches on a variety of sociological structures (political, religious, educational, legal, and familial). The way Warren took the reader in and out of these individual relationships was masterful. However, as an African American who grew up in the South, [I felt that] the narrative seemed all too familiar, and that had a nervous touch on my young soul."

The practical relevance of this novel's message to today's politics keeps bringing readers back to it. For some, the novel is prescient in the same way as dystopian novels such as George Orwell's *1984*. For Steve Beshear, *All the King's Men* raises questions about how to govern: "This book is as relevant today as it was when it was written in 1946," he says. "The book's practical value is that it asks two important questions: Why does one seek elected office, and—should you win that office—how are you going to govern?" The former governor of Kentucky concludes, "But what's noteworthy today is the anxiety (and in some cases the terror) of the collective American public as it watches those questions answered by those who've sought and won office on a high level in recent elections. The ramifications—for my state, this nation, and this world—are tremendous, as Warren foresaw." That question—How will one choose to govern?—is indeed a theme that the author himself would probably agree enlivens the novel's continuing relevance.

In his career as a journalist, Mark Neikirk has witnessed the relevance of the novel firsthand:

> I began reporting for a newspaper in 1979 as a full-time job and remained in that career for twenty-eight years. Across all of that time, whether I was observing politics at the local, state, or national level, Warren's portrayal remained vivid. His char-

acter, so set in the deep South of the twentieth century's first half, was present as real-life people in the century's second half. I remember a local mayor telling me once, "We all have big egos—we politicians. I do. You cannot run for office without a big ego. It's just part of what draws people to politics. But you are a public servant, too. You're trying to do some good for the people." Does that not sound like Willie Stark, called to service but also in dire need of public aplomb? And there [are] always, ever present, those Jack Burdens, young, idealistic, and on the road to disillusionment, though when you meet them they don't know what they don't know. The petty and not so petty crooks that populate politics were archetypes in the book, and then I saw them in real life.

"To understand politics," Neikirk concludes, "you can read many things. . . . But any literary canon of political 'texts' has to include *All the Kings Men*. It was revelatory when it was published and remains so today. The times change; the nature of man doesn't."

Judge Sara Combs considers the novel "a cross between biography and parable," with "a mission to instruct literarily rather than didactically." Judge Combs identifies the relevance clearly as an acknowledgment that historical sense and poetic sense are complementary: "It is a tale for all seasons of politics—what to expect when a half-mad, ruthless demagogue seizes power by manipulating the public psyche and then continues to draw strength and heightened ego stimulation from the very public that he has victimized by his own Sirens' song. It is the saga essentially of every dictator who has risen from populist roots to realize his dreams of empire. It crosses geographic borders and transcends social classes—from Lenin to Willie Stark to . . . ? We continue to provide nominees to carry on the series."

Justice Bill Cunningham affirms the book's relevance while

introducing another question that intrigues readers of *All the King's Men:* the ambiguities. Willie Stark, who has experienced poverty, wants to make good things happen for the people in his impoverished state. They need a hospital that will not turn away anyone in need. But to accomplish that ideal, the governor must make deals with corrupt people and thus compromise his dream in the process. What is the answer to this dilemma? Keep our hands and morals clean of corruption and not build the hospital so needed by sick and injured people? Compromise our ethics in pursuit of providing services to the suffering? What is the right answer? Justice Cunningham offers this perspective:

> The book will remain relevant as long as we have representative government of elective officeholders. I get a little something out of the book each time I read it. The story of Jack Burden and Willie Stark has led me to ask many youngsters this solid question about democracy. "Had you rather had an ineffective leader or a corrupt one?" We know the collateral damage which is caused by the Willie Stark kind is small consider[ing] the monumental damage which can be caused by ineffective but honest leaders. . . . As [with] most drama, I think the book leaves me with the notion that you probably have to be a little of both. Deals have to be made. Leaders sometimes have to wield power ruthlessly for the benefit of a larger good (i.e., Willie Stark and his state hospital). . . . In the end, if I had to sum up the book in a short phrase, I would say that it represents the moral ambiguities of good political leaders.

Cunningham says that being a little Machiavellian is like salt: "Every good and effective public servant has to use some of it. Did Willie Stark use it to the extreme? That's the intriguing question and power of Warren's book." That is the moral ambiguity.

As a former federal prosecutor for the US Department of Justice, Geoffrey Mearns explains that it is the ambiguities of the novel that most influenced his own work as a prosecutor. "There's a tendency of some prosecutors to be moralistic—'I'm good, and they're bad.' Now, [an individual's] conduct might be bad but that does not necessarily make them a bad person." It is this gray area of morality that draws Mearns to *All the King's Men*. During his career as a prosecutor, he encountered individuals who would certainly be considered bad. He was a member of the team that prosecuted organized crime boss John Gotti, and he served as the lead prosecutor in the case of Terry Nichols, one of the conspirators in the Oklahoma City bombing, which resulted in the deaths of 168 people, 19 of whom were children. Anyone would be justified in considering such individuals to be as bad as the horrible things they did, but Mearns is admirably thoughtful and reflective about his former work, noting that he was prosecuting the actions or bad decisions that such individuals had committed and made, but not the individuals themselves. Switching to a "lighter" topic, university politics, specifically the relationship between administration and faculty, Mearns (now speaking in his role as a university administrator) says that *All the King's Men* offers important lessons. Some administrators view faculty as too idealistic; some faculty view administrators as too pragmatic. As a result, he says, "Increasing divisions, skepticism, and downright hostilities that exist on some campuses impede our ability" to address problems. Mearns hopes for collegial relationships among opponents in government (he recalls Ronald Reagan and Tip O'Neill as a model of such a relationship), so that they can work together for the common good. He hopes for the same at universities. I went away from my conversation with Mr. Mearns with a greater appreciation for the way *All the King's Men* depicts the pragmatic individual oriented to action (the Boss) and the idealistic individual oriented to values (Adam Stanton). Both are essential, and both are potentially destructive. Either one without the other becomes an unbalanced extreme.

Other readers notice the novel's relevance to the political climate of the United States in the election year 2016 and thereafter.

Bill Goodman says, "An argument could be made in today's political climate that the novel resonates with themes present in the nation's mood; the common person, working-class whites, and political posturing seem to be playing out today just as [they] did seventy years ago. The deceitful shenanigans of yesterday might prove to be good study for power-hungry politicians of today."

Journalist Al Cross observes a developing significance for *All the King's Men,* in which the novel's application to current circumstances is evolving with time. "From the time it was published until I read it, about 1972, it was a useful cautionary tale for students who might get caught up in the postwar idealism about American democracy and discount the human elements. Then we had the Watergate burglary and revelation of all the illegal manipulations by Richard Nixon, on top of dissatisfaction about the Vietnam War (which we now know Nixon may have lengthened in order to get elected), and entered a more cynical age." Looking to today, Cross asks: "What lessons can government officials and citizens learn from the book? Human nature is the DNA of democracy; institutions are only frameworks constructed by flawed human beings, often to serve their own purposes. Every action has unforeseen consequences. You never know the whole story. There are limits to kinship and friendship. Democracy works best when leaders appeal to the better angels of our nature. It could be doomed by the likes of Huey Long, Willie Stark, and Donald Trump."[5]

For David Hawpe, *All the King's Men* is a cautionary tale, one that anticipates the rise of future Willie Starks long after its publication in 1946. "It's almost too obvious that *All the King's Men* anticipates the incendiary populism of today's national politics," says

Hawpe. "It is useful, too, in understanding the current Kentucky governor and his administration, in both positive and negative ways. The 'strong man' who identifies with 'the people'—meaning the 'little guy' or the 'average family'—is a familiar trope. The 'strong man' can do great things but also do great mischief and bring the people who vest in him to great grief. The novel makes that case, but it also illuminates the ossification of an old order, the petty privilege of an entrenched elite, the self-delusion of inherited privilege and power. Beyond all that, it simply tells a good story."

# 6

# How the Story Works

## The Role of "You"

*All the King's Men* somehow speaks to readers seventy years after its publication and counting. Literally, the novel speaks directly to you, the reader, from the very first line.

Literary critic Simone Vauthier noticed in the 1970s that "while the narrator in *All the King's Men* has received much critical attention, his partner in the act of communication has been rather neglected." That partner is the "narratee" or person listening to or reading Jack Burden's story. "The addressee," Vauthier points out, "is first to appear on the scene." That's "you" she's talking about.[1]

Let's revisit the opening again, where Jack Burden projects his voice and his gaze away from the car and toward an unnamed audience or reader: "To get there you follow Highway 58, going northeast out of the city, and it is a good highway and new. Or was new, that day we went up it. You look up the highway and it is straight for miles, coming at you, with the black line down the center coming at you and at you."[2] Notice the repetition of the word *you*. That is

Vauthier's crucial observation. "And on for two pages before the narrator-agent [Jack Burden] makes his appearance," she notes. "Thus it is the narratee who is first made to take the trip to Mason City."[3]

This observation of "you" is essential to answering the questions asked earlier: *In what way can* All the King's Men *be an anchor for us now? What does* All the King's Men *tell us about power and ethics at this particular time in the history of Kentucky or the United States?* Much that has been written about *All the King's Men* has focused on two characters: first, the object of the narrator's attention, Governor Willie Stark, the "Boss" and the "king" of the title, and, second, the narrator himself, Jack Burden, one of the "men" of the title. But we can expand our understanding of the first word in the title, *all.* All of the people who surround, assist, and support the king are not only those working immediately in his administration but also those women and men in the counties, cities, towns, and neighborhoods who vote for him, stick his name on the bumpers of their cars, and plant his name on the signs in their front lawns. Men of power—and those with power usually are male—do not seize or assume that power in vacuums. They are the products, the fulfillments, the creations of their historical moments. Though it goes without saying, it is worth repeating: no leaders in a democratic form of government can gain power without the voters who put them into office. A candidate gains such support by figuring out—either intentionally or intuitively—what his voters want to hear. In this way, a leader is, paradoxically, a follower.

We the readers, then, should read *All the King's Men* for what it shows us not only of the populist demagogue who rises to power in Robert Penn Warren's fictional world but also of the people around Willie Stark—Jack Burden, Sadie Burke, Anne Stanton, and those other named and unnamed individuals and crowds—all of those who are drawn to the Boss because he fulfills something for them. They are the characters with whom we can most readily identify.

Stark's power is ultimately attributable to all of those named and unnamed characters, just as our current leaders' powers are attributable to us. When Jack Burden speaks to the unidentified "you" who might or might not have voted for Willie Stark, he is speaking to all of us who will be presented with the option of voting for a Willie Stark in our own time.

Former *Louisville Courier-Journal* editor David Hawpe advocates focusing on how supporters are influenced by the very leader they support—a lesson personified by Jack Burden. "I think *All the King's Men* is a dark, disturbing work," Hawpe explains. "It's most obviously a look at how vulnerable any democracy is to cynicism, cronyism, and a lot of other unfortunate isms. What's easiest to lament is the fall of a tragic hero—Willie Stark's slow walk into moral failure." "But," Hawpe continues, "having spent a long career in journalism, what I see equally clearly is the moral hazard risked by the voyeur—in this instance, Jack Burden."[4] I like Hawpe's term *voyeur* to describe Jack and would enlarge that term to include all citizens—supporters and opponents—because we all are the voyeurs. Further, I embrace Tom Eblen's striking observation that "Jack Burden, the journalist turned political operative, has more in common with 'the Boss' than he wants to admit. He personifies the moral compromises many people make in search of success." By way of example, Eblen offers the episode early in the novel in which "Burden gives Stark a lesson in political rhetoric."[5] I examine that scene further in chapter 7. Here I only want to emphasize that Jack Burden exemplifies every citizen's potential attraction to a charismatic political figure. We justify our political choices and make excuses for them when their flaws show. All voters make moral compromises in their search for political success.

*All the King's Men* is a cautionary tale, warning Americans that we citizens must beware of our need to seek fulfillment in political heroes. We must hold our elected leaders accountable, of course, but we must also hold ourselves accountable. We must understand how their rhetoric works so that we can notice how it works on us. The techniques of rhetoric and persuasion must be taught in high school and college courses in English, language arts, speech, history, and political science so that students can put a name to the techniques that all politicians use, especially demagogic politicians. An examination of some key moments in *All the King's Men* illuminates how the populist demagogue, Willie Stark, uses language—and, more to the point, how the people around him are used by his language.

# 7

# The Rhetoric of the Populist Demagogue

## "He Could T-t-talk so Good"

The term *demagogue* refers to a leader who gains power by appealing to strong emotion and prejudices and may be extended to include one who gains power through false claims or empty promises. As we have seen, the term is often applied in discussions of Willie Stark. That first definition—referencing emotions and prejudices—seems fitting: Willie reminds his audiences that they are poor, uneducated "hicks" who are justified in their hard-earned feelings of resentment against the stereotypical, urban, business, and political elites in the state's power centers. He is, in this regard, like politicians who assure their audiences that they are the "real" Americans. These kinds of appeals can be effective because they bolster the identities of socially, educationally, and economically vulnerable listeners. Applying the extended definition of the term *demagogue* to Willie Stark seems more open to debate. Are his claims false and his promises empty?

Governor Stark genuinely intends to provide infrastructure to improve the health and raise the economic levels of and educational opportunities for the poor people of his state. His promises form more than a stratagem to get elected; they cohere into a program. Stark's populism unifies around an ideological core. His promises to his constituents are not empty (his promises to the women in his life are another matter), but those promises do exact some high prices. Whatever kind of demagogue he is, however, he shares the essential trait of all demagogues: skill in public speaking. Public speech is the sine qua non of demagoguery.

Willie's skill as a speaker is a major element of his character development. It appears most emphatically in the final chapter of the novel, which functions as an extended coda or final act. Jack revisits all of the major and a few of the minor characters to make sense of Willie's life and his own life as well. Essentially, he struggles to answer the unasked questions: *What happened?* and *Where do I go from here?* One of the quieter players he encounters—by accident, actually—is Sugar-Boy in the library newspaper room. Willie's faithful subordinate, Sugar-Boy appears directionless in the aftermath of the assassination: "'He could t-t-talk so good,'" he half-mumbles, stuttering. "'The B-B-Boss could. Couldn't nobody t-t-talk like him. When he m-m-made a speech and ev-ev-everybody y-y-yelled, it looked 1-1-like something was gonna b-b-burst inside y-y-you.' . . . 'Sure,' I agreed, 'he was a great talker.'"[1]

That is a powerful last line—a little slick, perhaps—because the expression "good talker" goes beyond acknowledging someone's skill with the spoken word to imply that this person is scheming, shrewd, duplicitous, and deceptive. Jack relates Sugar-Boy's history to the reader. Sugar-Boy was born in Irish Town, bullied by the bigger kids, excluded from neighborhood baseball games, made the object of name calling, designated the gofer to fetch baseball bats and drinks for the other boys, who bossed him, as he would later be a gofer for the Boss himself. But Sugar-Boy can drive and shoot a gun, so one day he found himself working for the governor, who considered his talents useful.

The line "He could t-t-talk so good" is so significant that in the stage version of *All the King's Men* (1959) Warren has Sugar-Boy say it in the prologue and again in act 3, where it is literally the final line of the play.[2] Sugar-Boy is impressionable and vulnerable; the Boss gives him what he needs: a sense of self-worth. With the Boss, he gets to play and be a tough guy, a member of a team of winners. Sugar-Boy is seduced by Willie's ability to speak in a way that appeals to Sugar-Boy's needs. The Boss, like every successful political leader, knows intuitively how to fulfill the needs of the people around him. Those needs might be material (e.g., jobs, lower taxes) or physical (e.g., food, housing, health care) or emotional (e.g., affirmation of identity, attitude, ideology). Whatever the needs, they are addressed initially through language because power starts with language, power is pursued through language, and, in the end, the deal is closed through language.[3]

Language includes visuals. In the iconic first chapter, the car heading to Willie's childhood home for the photo session stops at the local drugstore. Willie is greeted with people calling his name. A large picture of him hangs above the soda fountain. Known to the locals by his first name rather than by his title, his presence preceded by a larger-than-life picture and a slogan announcing his empathy with "the people," Willie makes a populist, antielitist appeal before he even speaks a word.[4]

Then he sees one of his constituents, Old Leather-Face. They shake hands, and Willie calls him by his first name, Malaciah. The man's son, Willie learns, is in legal trouble due to a fight that resulted in the other fellow's death. Willie sympathizes. (Later, back in the car, Willie will direct Jack to arrange for an attorney to represent Malaciah's son but to do so in a way that ensures that the link back to the governor will be untraceable.) Quietly to Doc behind the counter, Willie asks for his order in a manner hinting that he wants it to be hurried up. It's all on the house, of course. Every element of the scene demonstrates the people's familiarity with him and his accessibility to them. But as his behind-the-scenes comments suggest, his words and actions together form a public performance for Willie Stark.

That performance continues with the first in a series of speeches that we might call *nonspeeches* because they begin with Willie announcing that he is not going to give a speech. The crowd outside the drugstore begins yelling for a speech, to which Willie remarks only to those in the drugstore that he came not to make speeches but to visit his father. Neither statement is quite true; Willie is returning primarily to use his father's house as a backdrop to depict himself, the candidate, as a family man for the photo shoot. But for the moment he leaves the drugstore, with the crowd following him. Jack describes him as a man walking alone but apparently aware that the crowd is closing behind him. Jack notices in Willie's face the signs of an oncoming speech that he has surely seen many times before. Then Willie begins a "nonspeech" by saying, "I'm not going to make any speech." These lines are representative of the pattern of phrases that Willie will repeat throughout the speech. After he declares that he will not give a speech, what follows is, of course, a speech. What Willie is doing here is an example of *paralepsis* (also called *apophasis*), a strategy of rhetoric, especially political rhetoric, in which a speaker raises a subject by claiming that he or she will not raise the subject. This technique is usually employed for a subversive ad hominem attack, a personal accusation against one campaigner by another. For example, a candidate might say, "I don't want to attack my opponent for his inexperience." Or "Some people accuse my opponent of dishonesty, but I won't stoop that low." Or "I could easily say X, but if I did, the media would jump all over me, so I won't say X." The point *is* communicated by the very act of declaring that the point will *not* be communicated. Paralepsis is a sly tactic when it comes with good intentions but a dishonest one when the intentions are less than well meaning. Invoking a speech in the very act of denying it, Willie is being tactical in the way he engages with his audience.

The speech Willie gives is not a scheduled one, certainly; it is a speech of opportunity, a seizing of the moment, but he turns that moment to his own rhetorical and political benefit. The message of the speech is the simple fact that he has come home. After alluding to the book of Proverbs and to politicians who are always asking for money or votes, Willie states, "But I'm not a politician today. I'm taking the day off. I'm not even going to ask you to vote for me."[5]

When Willie says, "I'm not a politician today," he is, of course, being a politician. It is prudent to keep in mind that no politician plays politics more than the one who accuses his opponents of playing politics. Every utterance in politics is a power play. The biblical references, the mention of his father and down-home cooking, the declarations that he is not a politician and not giving a speech— every one of these statements serves a political purpose: to persuade the people that he, Governor Stark, is just Willie, one of *them*, not one of those detached, elitist politicians. He presents himself as the local boy who made good, which, by the way, is true. But he constructs and maintains an image of himself not as a politician coming to them from outside their community but rather as a member of their community returning to them. He serves as an aspirational symbol for them.

"Willie knows his power originates in the will of the electorate," Frank Fury argues in an article about sports, power, and politics in the novel, "and, because of this knowledge, he appeals to their sense of community and the vicarious thrill they experience as a result of the satisfaction of seeing a member of the community speak for them. The vibrant and charismatic energy of his speeches elicits frenzied reactions from the crowds." Fury provides a description of Willie as "the model of the American Dream of success" and the perceptive observation that Willie is a living image of his own dirt metaphor (someone who literally worked in the dirt):

> Traditionally, the American hero of legend and folklore is a self-made achiever. He rises from obscurity and through adversity to the apex of achievement. Warren uses the metaphor of "dirt" as a starting point to emphasize the notion that the success of both the father and the son grows organically from the "common ground" on which we all live. Willie's association with the image of dirt proves multivalent. He will use the "dirt" metaphor to illustrate his own philosophy that in order to make good out of bad, one must start amidst the dirt and make progress from it.[6]

Willie's speaking style is, then, the populist style in rhetoric. In the *Virginia Quarterly Review,* Sanford Pinsker describes contemporary populism as "less a sharply defined political movement, as was the Populist Movement of the 1890s," and more "a sensibility, one that amazingly enough, now gets equal time on both sides of the aisle." Pinsker calls this attitude "small-*p* populism," which is expressed by style of clothes, music, and venues that a politician chooses for campaigning. Consider the candidates whose policies are not Populist (capital P) but whose cowboy boots, country music themes, and appearances at county fairs suggest otherwise (populist with the small *p*). For Pinsker, the "poster child[ren] for small-*p* populism" are Huey Long and, by extension, Willie Stark.[7]

This is not to say that the Long/Stark political, economic, and infrastructure programs were not populist. Willie Stark is authentically populist in the sense that he seeks to represent the economic interests of the common people living in rural areas and working the land for a living. But a political movement is represented by a style that conveys its substance. Populism for Willie Stark is a style as well as an ideology or a program. His appeals to the beliefs, values, and homegrown commonsense wisdom of the people, in contrast to what are assumed to be the affected, rootless values of the city elite, emerge from the authenticity of his own background as one of those same people. But those appeals also function as his rhetorical style. It is the populist style that Willie is using when he tells the crowd that he is not a politician giving a speech. His audience most likely understands it to mean that he is not going to read to them from a sheet of paper upon which text has been written, revised, edited, and polished for him by his staff. He is not going to recite remarks that have been prepared and rehearsed in advance. The extemporaneous utterance, it is assumed, will be something more authentic. This assumption about political speech, heard in the criticism that some politicians have received for their reliance on notes or teleprompters, misses a crucial quality of the writing and speaking process. It ironically considers speech less authentic when the speaker has carefully considered and shaped the message to make it express, as accurately as possible—that is, as authentically as possible—the speaker's intent. Any preparation is suspected to be overpreparation.

The assumption also misses a crucial quality of extemporaneous political speech: it is not necessarily truly extemporaneous. The populist style is a genre or inventory of conventions that Stark or any populist speaker can draw upon at any time. Certain elements of the spoken language—word choice, references, images, length of sentences, colloquialisms, folksy expressions and pronunciations—construct the populist style. Certain elements of performance—facial expressions, gestures, vocal tone, and demeanor—enact the populist style. Stark creates a mental storage room of populist speech—the references to his father and the Bible as well as his insistence that he is not a politician. He is well prepared to speak without preparation.

Let's look at one more scene depicting populist rhetoric and thoroughly prepared spontaneity. This time, the occasion is not a speech but the staging of a campaign photograph.

The time of the narration is 1939, but the story itself is a recollection from 1936, well into Stark's political rise. The context is his reelection campaign for governor: a photo op that has been arranged to depict the governor as a family man relaxing at home with his wife, his son, his elderly dad, and his dog, too. Of course, by this time, the governor's attachment to home has already been deteriorating. He has been cheating repeatedly on his wife, Lucy, and he has been emotionally separating from his son, his own father, and, while we're at it, even from his dog. For the nonexistent happy family scene to materialize for this photo, someone is going to have to make it all happen.

The photo is thus staged, a work of pure fiction. Jack speculates that the house has intentionally not been painted because the neighbors would become suspicious and speculate about how Old Man Stark got the money for such a fancy paint job—perhaps from his son in the governor's mansion? Jack notes that the house actually does have some nice improvements, including indoor plumbing, but that sort of thing is not visible from the road. This kind of populist style on the part of Old Man Stark is probably not intentional, in Jack's estimation, but it is no less politically convenient. Jack remarks on the usefulness of the earthy scenery: an unpainted house will make for a better picture to depict the governor as coming from modest beginnings. The photographer positions his subjects on the front porch of the house and then gets a great idea. Or maybe not so great. "'The dog,' he said, 'get the dog in there with you, Governor. You be petting the dog or something.'"[8]

A problem arises. The dog, Buck, lacks the interest or the stamina to come to Willie when he is called. This is an affront to Willie as the dog's trusted master. "The Boss looked at me, and I knew what I was paid to do. 'Jack,' the Boss said, 'get the hairy bastard up here and make him look like he was glad to see me.'" Jack and a couple of other men try to heave the uncooperative canine into position, which doesn't work, so they literally drag him up to the Boss and lay "the faithful head" on the Boss's leg.[9]

Buck's disinterest is the culmination of this farcical fiction being manufactured by the governor's aides. The happy-family picture will represent the candidate as family man to the voters and will be presented to the public as an image of the governor's authenticity, but it is an artificial portrait of an artificial moment. An argument can be made that Willie Stark is authentically a man of the people and a populist, but when necessary, he can fake the sincerity.

# 8

# The Pandering Populist

## "Don't Try to Improve Their Minds"

Willie Stark didn't start out as a fake. He had to learn how to appeal to the people, and the way to do that was to appeal to himself. The humiliation of being used by the state government "big boys" for their own purposes steered him toward sympathy with the rural people, who were being disserved by the political establishment. This humiliation initiated a key moment in his career that led to the emergence of his populist voice.

As a reporter for the *Chronicle,* Jack was assigned to cover Willie's first campaign for governor. Jack explains to us that at that time Willie's speeches were recitations of statistics and data points that he would rehearse in his hotel room as if he were preparing some great oration. While delivering the speeches, he would fumble with sheets of the papers filled with all the data about his tax program or road program. The speeches were boring and ignored.

Then, as Tom Eblen describes the scene, "Burden gives Stark a lesson in political rhetoric that, sadly, is as relevant today as it was then."[1] Burden's advice to Stark is to keep his speeches simple and limited to slogans—to stop talking about issues and start delivering talking points—in order to appeal not to the intellect but to the emotions. This part of the scene is significant and well known among the novel's readers: "You tell 'em too much. Just tell 'em you're gonna soak the fat boys, and forget the rest of the tax stuff. . . . Hell, make 'em cry, make 'em laugh. . . . Or make 'em mad. . . . It's up to you to give 'em something to stir 'em up and make 'em feel alive again. Just for half an hour. That's what they come for. Tell 'em anything. But for Sweet Jesus' sake don't try to improve their minds."[2]

In this scene, which Michael Washburn of Louisville Public Radio calls "the novel's most pivotal scene," Jack is Willie Stark's "fixer," and Willie is the "neophyte."[3] The character Jack Burden could be any one of today's celebrity campaign strategists—James Carville, Lee Atwater, Mary Matalin, Karl Rove, Ken Mehlman, David Plouffe, Jim Messina, or Kellyanne Conway—who script, stage, prepare, and rehearse their candidates for cable television interviews and debate performances and, it must be allowed, for the "spontaneous" moments as well. In the sound bites and photo ops of campaign advertisements and speeches, we see for ourselves candidates who "don't try to improve their minds."

The result of putting this advice to practice for Willie Stark is a breakout speech—a "nonspeech"—in which he discovers his populist voice after his aide, Sadie Burke, reveals to him that he is being used by the party establishment only to split the vote. He finds that voice in a sense of shared victimization and resentment with his audience. Standing on the platform humiliated and disoriented (as well as hung over from an atypical binge the previous night), Willie begins by theatrically tossing the written speech aside and telling the story of his own life, a story crafted to connect to the lives of his listeners.[4]

In a performance of populist rhetoric, Willie first assures his audience that their identity is the true identity of the state or nation, that they are the "real people," which by definition marginalizes or excludes anyone else (such as big-city elites). He and they are on the same team. "You are the state," he declares. Second, he affirms that his listeners are well informed and smart and therefore require no instruction from government or any intermediary (such as the media or educational institutions). He flatters their sense of self-esteem and self-importance. "You know what you need," he tells them. Third, as we have seen, he presents himself as authentic, not needing any prepared remarks (such as notes or full text), announcing, "I'm not going to read you any speech." Instead he will tell them a story, which is, of course, going to be a speech, but in using narrative rather than facts and figures, he makes himself and his program accessible to the audience. As any nonprofit organization raising funds knows, a powerful story is much more effective than statistics. It makes the audience feel something. He will not *read;* rather, he will *tell.* The story is "about a red-neck, like you all." Thus begins Willie's autobiographical account of himself as a hick, getting up early to milk cows and walk to a one-room schoolhouse and eventually deciding to make something of himself by studying law.[5]

Continuing his third-person story about "the hick," Willie turns the "plot" to reveal how he was used by the political elites, represented by Tiny Duffy on that very stage, the same ones responsible for the political corruption that resulted in the injuries of children at the schoolhouse due to faulty construction materials. As the crowd turns against Duffy, Willie's political capital rises. He has successfully wedged a division between his audience and the political establishment, persuading them to come to him for solidarity. "Populism preys on people's feelings of disenchantment and victimization at the hands of elites," Michael Washburn says. "And rather than harness those feelings to create broad solidarity, populism forges angry confederacies, usually along class and racial lines, and encourages a caustic defensiveness from folks held in the thrashing populist eddy."[6] From this major, career-jump-starting speech, Harold Woodell notes, "[Stark] stumps the state with speeches beginning with the address, 'Friends, red-necks, suckers, and fellow hicks,' that unite him and listeners in a common cause—the overthrow of the entrenched political establishment and the status quo the Old Boys represent. This identification of a common enemy will prove to be a powerful tool, as Stark becomes a demagogue to bend the will of the people to his own."[7]

The common cause, we should note, is not merely the stuff of speech rhetoric, though. It exists in a very real way as a program of reform and public services. Joyce Carol Oates suggests, "We expect to learn that Stark is a sham, a manipulator of credulous voters, but in fact Stark is respectful of his rowdy redneck constituency." He is respectful in using emotional appeals not only to convince voters but also to enact a program on behalf of those voters.[8] As Steven D. Ealy observes, "It is during this campaign that Willie articulates a political program for the first time, a program that could be characterized as a southern populist platform." Such a platform might be tax reform, road improvements, efficient administration, and better schools, all especially implemented in the rural areas. But in addition to forming the core of policy for his campaign and later for his administration, his speeches demonstrate what Ealy calls "redneck resentment not as something incidental to his campaign, but as its emotional core."[9]

Stark returns to that "emotional core" of "redneck resentment" like a bank account that he can draw upon when he needs political advantage. When impeachment proceedings begin, he travels around the state (always in the car speeding at eighty miles an hour) to give speeches that begin informally, almost as if they were unprepared remarks. After some name-calling directed at his political adversaries, he affirms solidity with his audience, telling them that he needs to leave the capital occasionally to see the real people.

Stark uses folksy words and cadences, assuring his audience of their authentic identity and intelligence apart from the distanced elites and allying himself with them. What he says features all the elements of populist rhetoric that he learned earlier in his career.[10]

What follows is a call-and-response as Willie asks the people if he has disappointed them, and they answer with roars of approval. The scene takes on the tone of a revival. Later, on the night he wins the impeachment vote, the crowds will be standing in front of the state capitol building chanting his name.[11] At such moments, Joyce Carol Oates proposes, "it could as easily be a lynching that Willie Stark is rousing his followers to commit as a more abstract assault upon the monied elite of the state." In the second film version, director and screenwriter Steven Zaillian ratchets up the crowd scenes to an even more intense level. During the campaign, Stark directs the crowd's anger against the elites and the establishment politicians, controlling the state capital with chants such as "Nail 'em up!" The stage version by Warren produced in 1959 ratchets the intensity further with the chant "Kill 'em!"[12]

In both style and substance, Willie Stark plays to and foments the crowds' distrust of the institutions that run the state. As Ron Elving notes, "What has Willie done? He's won elections as an outsider and smashed the old power structure in the capital. He's built roads and bridges, hospitals and schools. And he's eliminated every rival for power and every competing authority."[13] Notice the verbs that Zaillian uses in his script and Elving in his description: *nail, win, smash*. Willie Stark takes the crowd along a disturbingly sharp edge of speech that might be understood, on the one hand, as metaphorical but might as easily be understood, on the other hand, by some of his most loyal "base" supporters as a call for actual violence against political opponents. Willie Stark is not a political leader in some dystopian, placeless world that exists only in fiction, nor is he a political leader in Venezuela or Zimbabwe or Russia. The setting is the United States, which makes the implications even more unsettling. In the United States, violence against political opposition has been limited to the actions of individual followers, such as an attempted assassination or, more typically, the vandalism of a campaign headquarters or an assault upon individual supporters or protestors. Such acts are always extrajudicial and usually condemned by political leaders. We do not have a dark, contemporary tradition of Willie Stark–like politicians condoning such actions or, worse, encouraging them.

For Woodell, such scenes present "a textbook case of rabble-rousing" in which "Stark uses demagogic rhetoric as a weapon to inflame the plain folk against his enemies in the capital." On this point, Woodell offers insights. "Warren has shown how the dynamics of demagoguery work to lead a man like Willie Stark to gain control of the masses through calculating techniques of manipulation. Following a pattern common to other powerful rulers, Stark identifies with the common people, understands their needs, attacks a common enemy, and uses his power to gain total control of state politics." However, "in the end, it is Stark's failure to account for the irrational in human conduct that brings about his demise."[14] His rhetorical power makes his political power possible, but the limitation of that power will check his ambitions. He can control entire crowds, but he cannot control the individuals he hurts in his exercise of power. It is not the voting populace but one of those individuals who will bring his aspirations to an end. The problem for Willie Stark, as it is for all demagogues, is that he believes he can control history, but he cannot.

# 9

# The King's Man

## "Who Do I Work For?"

In chapter 8, we considered the importance of Willie Stark's followers in *All the King's Men*. Primary among them is the one who follows his story more closely than anyone else: Willie's narrator, Jack Burden. In various interviews, Warren explained the genesis of the Jack Burden character. He first appeared in the precursor to the novel: the verse drama titled *Proud Flesh,* written in the 1930s. In the assassination scene, act 5, scene 1, a character appears who is simply called "Friend." As Dr. Amos (precursor to Adam Stanton) waits armed in the corridor, this "Friend" appears, a man described in the stage directions as "shabbily and loosely dressed," with papers shoved into his coat, "a raincoat slung over one arm," and "hat jammed jauntily on the back of his head." "He is a reporter, an old friend" of the assassin. They chat. "I'll be damned. . . . How are you?" and so forth. It's a pause in the dramatic tension. In an interview with fellow southern writer Flannery O'Connor, Warren said that this moment initially created "kind of a hold, you know, until the action could happen . . . a dramatic need of fiction, a need of pace." But then "when the novel idea started out some years later . . . I thought on an idle Sunday afternoon: that newspaperman might be useful. The moment of nostalgia might be made into some kind of feeling by which to tell the story. That was how he [Jack Burden] got in there [the novel]. I remember that distinctly."[1]

As Warren transformed this drama into novel form, he realized the necessity of having a character who would function as a specific device—a follower who would have his own story in counterpoint to the story of Willie Stark. He realized that Jack Burden could play this role: "My play [*Proud Flesh*] is, indeed, about power, its genesis and the temptations it carries for both leader and follower; but I wanted my story to be personal rather than political. I wanted the issues to come to crisis in personal terms. I wanted to indicate some interplay, as it were, between the public, political story and the private, ethical one: a mirror held up to a mirror. . . . I suppose that what I wanted was the 'follower' to go with my 'leader.'"[2] Among "all the king's men," Jack is the central "king's man." His conflicting professional functions make him distinctive from the other "king's men and women." Initially he is a journalist, his role being to remain on the margins to report the action. Then he works as an aide to Willie, his role as a political operative putting him in the center of the action. He transitions from neutrality to involvement. In our own time, we see a blurred line separating politics and news. Cable television news pundits drop their microphones to work in presidential campaigns, and presidential aides sign contracts with cable news organizations. Decades earlier, Warren had created Jack Burden as a character who crosses the boundary between reporting the news and making the news.

Jack reveals that he is a reporter at the same time he tells us how he was introduced to Willie. The passing sight of the brick schoolhouse during that nighttime car trip in 1936 in the first chap-

ter leads Jack to remember how he and Willie first met fourteen
years earlier, in 1922. Willie was the Mason County treasurer, working on the bond issue for the schoolhouse, and Jack was in the back
room of Slade's pool hall waiting with Tiny Duffy to talk to Deputy
Sheriff Alex Michel. Jack was using Tiny Duffy to get the interview
with Alex Michel because Jack's employer, the *Chronicle,* was supporting Governor Joe Harrison, Duffy's boss.

We next see Jack at work as a reporter in chapter 2 when the
managing editor of the *Chronicle* sends him to Mason City to investigate Willie's role in the schoolhouse bond issue. This is the issue
that will eventually put the name "Willie Stark" on the political
map because he had tried to keep the construction contracts hon-
est, but the corruption proceeded anyway, resulting in shoddy construction of the school and eventually in a structural failure that
caused the deaths and injuries of several children. Jack arrives in
Mason City to investigate and after a meal at the Mason City Café
joins some of the old-timers on a bench outside the harness shop. He
primes the bull session by interjecting himself into the conversation.
He discovers that people are aware that Willie is the one slowing
down the project because he wants the city to take the low bid. But
some of the white citizens fear that the low bid will mean the hiring
of black workers at the expense of white workers.

At the courthouse, Jack encounters a stonewalling sheriff
reluctant to help an outsider reporter rooting around, but through
persistence Jack is able to meet one of the commissioners, Dolph
Pillsbury, for another round of stonewalling. Despite their efforts
to block Jack's investigation, these men do reveal sufficient bits of
information to confirm to him that he is on the trail of a story worth
digging into. Talking with Willie gives Jack the story of a kickback
scheme: the contract will be handed to a higher-bidding company
that is partially owned by Pillsbury's brother-in-law and uses cheap
convict labor rather than to the lower-bidding company that would

use black labor. The dirty deal will be sold to the public behind the distraction of white resentment. Willie gets no cooperation from the local newspaper in Mason City, the *Messenger,* so he fights the corruption by distributing handbills and talking with citizens on his own.

Working for the *Chronicle* outside Mason City, Jack is part of an out-of-town machinery that raises Willie's profile statewide. He describes the newspaper's role in preparing the way for Willie's political reform, or, as he says, "setting the stage and preparing the backdrop for the real show." Mason County, Jack explains, is in the newspaper's sights because Willie is giving "the touch of drama to the sordid tale."[3] Notice the theater terminology Jack uses here. A populist program promising reform will be a *show* in front of a *backdrop* on a *stage* set by the newspaper's *tale* of corruption that Willie invigorates with a sense of *drama.* It's all a narrative, with the word *tale* suggesting a particularly imaginative narrative. To paraphrase Shakespeare, "All the political world's a stage."

Jack's transition from reporter to political aide, then, is not abrupt. It is a shift from one part of the stage to another, trading one role in the dramatis personae for another. That shift will occur at the end of chapter 2, when he resigns his job at the *Chronicle* and accepts a job offer from the newly elected governor, Willie Stark. But Jack goes through a period of middle passage when Jack as reporter is covering Willie's first campaign for governor. That is the campaign when Jack gives Willie advice about how to give a speech ("For Sweet Jesus' sake don't try to improve their minds") in the pivotal scene already discussed in chapter 8. What motivated Jack to school Willie in political public speaking? Let's go back a couple of pages before that moment. Jack, on assignment for the newspaper to cover the campaign, is listening to Willie practice his speeches in the adjoining hotel room. Jack describes his job not as "I was covering his campaign" but this way: "I was supposed to cover his campaign."[4] Already Jack is implying that his journalistic stance is not neutral, the word *supposed* suggesting that perhaps he might not be covering the campaign as a reporter. He feels sorry for Willie and, as we have seen, gives him free advice for improving his campaign speeches. That scene, then, functions as a kind of impromptu job interview in which Jack demonstrates his usefulness as a future assistant to the future officeholder. Jack in the hotel with Willie is like the pool reporter on the campaign bus, getting close to the candidate he is covering.

That scene in the hotel room begins to set the stage and prepare the backdrop for the real show of Jack abandoning all pretense of neutrality, quitting his newspaper job, and ultimately accepting the job offer from Willie. But one more career move further sets the stage. Jack tells us that he is now a "pundit"; his job description has shifted from providing reports to providing commentary. This is what lands him into a conflict with the newspaper's editor. Jack is writing columns at odds with the newspaper's decision to support Sam MacMurfee, Willie's corrupt opponent. When the newspaper's editor suggests that Jack is trying to help Willie "just because that Stark happens to be a friend of yours," Jack replies, "He's no friend of mine," insisting on his neutrality. He and the *Chronicle* part ways.[5]

The political narrative pauses for a few pages. Jack enters a period that he refers to as his "Great Sleep." He goes to movies, bars, the country club. He returns home and visits his old friends, Adam Stanton and Anne Stanton. But then the phone rings. It's Sadie Burke. Willie now has a new name, "the Boss," and he wants to talk with Jack. Willie offers Jack a job.

> "Who do I work for? The state?"
> "Hell, no. Me."[6]

This chilling exchange demonstrates a shift in loyalties from the body politic to the politician. Jack is asked not to work as an aide on behalf of the people of the state or the government that is supposed to function in their best interests, but only on behalf of Willie Stark personally. His off-the-books job consists of whatever murky duties Willie requires at each political moment. Willie's priority is himself—his own power, his own image. In accepting the job offer, Jack Burden becomes the king's man.

Willie's priority of himself over the state plays out in situations such as the nonfiring of Byram White, the state employee who attempts to embezzle funds from the government. Rather than protecting the state's interests by demanding White's immediate resignation and prosecution, Stark fears that his own image and power might be damaged if the media, the public, and political opponents were to find out about the incident. He covers up the crime and simultaneously gains leverage against White for future favors.

The contemporary reader might take Governor Willie Stark as a warning against demagogues who prioritize loyalty to their own personal interests above loyalty to the law, ethics, and the people they are supposed to serve. The contemporary reader might take Jack Burden as a representative of such a leader's supporters. They have faith in the promises made by their Willie Starks, and they vote in earnest, but they discover that they have sold out their own interests. Jack Burden stands as the symbol of such supporters. The harm caused to others by Jack's investigation of Judge Irwin on behalf of "the Boss" redounds upon Jack himself in ways he could not have predicted. He ends up smearing himself with the dirt he digs up.

Many literary critics and Warren scholars who have studied the novel have noticed Jack's metamorphosis from detached reporter to involved operative. Norton Girault observes that "the manner in which he reconstructs the story gives the reader an insight into Jack's experience." Thomas Daniel Young characterizes that manner as smart-alecky on the exterior but not fooling anyone: "Although Jack's wisecracking manner makes him seem detached from what he is observing, the reader is aware that he is deeply and profoundly affected." Robert Heilman agrees that Jack's tone suggests a narrator who is "sardonic in a detachment closer to alienation than objectivity."[7] As a form of rejection, alienation implies attachment.

Some critics have noted that Jack's attempts at self-alienation fail as he becomes more personally involved in the action he narrates. Situating Jack within a larger literary tradition, James Justus states: "Call him Ishmael or Carraway, Burden is another in a long line of American narrators who by dint of their special positions in the stories they tell end by telling their own stories as well. . . . It is Burden's revelation of [Willie Stark's] progress that is the experience of the book," but Jack Burden discovers his own identity through the rise and fall of Willie Stark and through "his articulation of those meanings in a long I-narration." Leonard Casper detects that "as a student of history, a reporter, and a political researcher, [Jack Burden] tries to perfect neutrality. Yet in each capacity he becomes more and more deeply, personally involved."[8]

In the stage version of *All the King's Men,* Warren emphasizes Jack's changing relationship to the narrative by situating the actor who plays Jack physically on the stage for every scene but standing on the margins of the action. According to the stage directions, "During the entire play [Jack] is always present, watching, from one point of vantage or another, the course of the action." In the second act, a character called "Professor" (who provides rebuttals to Jack's observations on the action) confronts Jack's attraction to Willie and challenges Jack's attempts to remain aloof: "Being incapable of action in your own confused and wasted life, you had a romantic admiration for action. Oh, you fancied the role of the cynical observer, but deep inside—."[9]

Jack's shift from ostensible neutrality to personal involvement is reflected in the narrative he relates in chapter 4, the story of Cass Mastern. This chapter is an interpolated narrative that could be excerpted from the novel to stand on its own as a short story. In fact, Warren originally published it separately in a journal and refigured it as a script for a stage performance. In its own right, it is an engrossing story. But it is deeply intertwined with the novel and becomes even more engrossing in what it reveals about the development of Jack Burden.

In this chapter, Jack tells the story of himself as a graduate student in history, researching and writing the story of his mid-nineteenth-century ancestor Cass Mastern. Cass in turn tells his own story in his personal journal. Unlike his pragmatic and materialist brother, Gilbert, Cass is a romantic figure. He has an affair with Annabelle, the wife of his best friend, Duncan Trice. Duncan commits suicide after discovering the affair, leaving a subtle clue (his wedding ring on his pillow) to communicate that knowledge to Annabelle. Complicating the situation, Annabelle has sold an enslaved woman, Phebe, down the river into the harshest conditions of slavery because Phebe knows the secret and Annabelle cannot bear the shame she feels every time Phebe looks at her. Overcome by guilt for the death of Duncan and the horror that awaits Phebe, Cass frees all of his own slaves and tries to locate and free Phebe. Unsuccessful, he enlists in the Confederate army with the intent of getting himself killed, a kind of suicide by war to expiate his sins. This part of the journal ends up having a significant effect upon Jack. He comments on the Cass Mastern material: "I have said that Jack Burden could not put down the facts about Cass Mastern's world because he did not know Cass Mastern. Jack Burden did not say definitely to himself why he did not know Cass Mastern. But I (who am what Jack Burden became) look back now, years later, and try to say why."[10] Jack uses his own name and the third-person pronoun *he* to describe himself as if he is talking about another person, but then he uses the first-person pronoun *I* to take ownership of his story. His use of *I* indicates that he is shedding his pose as the neutral reporter-narrator and is now participating in the story. It is as if he is beginning to write his own autobiography.[11]

This passage is representative of many other passages that the reader will find in *All the King's Men,* where Jack vacillates between referring to himself in the third person and referring to himself in the first person. The shift in pronoun is significant because it reflects a taking of ownership or responsibility. If I am referring to myself by my name, it is as if I am another person detached from my own behavior, but if I speak of myself as "I," then I am taking responsibility. This shift in pronoun thus reflects the moral lesson Jack learns from his historical research into the Cass Mastern story. As I have argued in *Making History: The Biographical Narratives of Robert Penn Warren,* the Cass Mastern chapter is central to the novel because it delivers to Jack a mirror image of his own responsibility. "Cass eventually accepts responsibility for the unintended consequences of his actions. He acknowledges his own and all other individuals' mutual participation in history. But the Cass Mastern chapter also tells the story of Jack Burden" because it is Cass's journal that ultimately compels Jack to consider his own responsibility for the consequences of his service to the Boss. This is why Jack decides to tell the story of Willie Stark. As a graduate student, Jack put aside his research into Cass Mastern, but after the conclusion of Willie's story he is ready to resume that project. As I explain in *Making History,* "From Mastern's narrative Burden learns how to write the narrative of Willie Stark. We might question whether the narrative of Stark would even exist had Burden not read Mastern's journal, because from that text Burden learns to place himself into history." Just as Mastern's journal is his confession, "the novel is Burden's confession. He publishes his errors and articulates his responsibility."[12]

Because Cass writes that "the vibration set up in the whole fabric of the world by my act had spread infinitely," Jack develops a spider web analogy to explain his theory of responsibility: "Cass

Mastern lived for a few years and in that time he learned that the world is all of one piece. He learned that the world is like an enormous spider web and if you touch it, however lightly, at any point, the vibration ripples to the remotest perimeter. . . . It does not matter whether or not you meant to brush the web of things."[13] Warren is articulating an understanding of all human actions as interrelated in a network of intended and unintended causes and effects. It is beyond the comprehension or control of any human being to foresee all effects or even to know when an action might function as the cause of some near or faraway effect. L. Hugh Moore, in his study of Warren as a writer of history, offers a powerful interpretation of the web analogy: "This theory of historical interrelatedness should not be interpreted as implying a moral plan to the universe, for there is nothing orderly, logical, planned, or predictable about the operation of the web of history. Warren, however, argues that this web necessitates man's acceptance of complete responsibility for his every act beyond any rational intention and for the mere fact of his existence, for in Warren' world-view even the best of intentions can bring about disastrous consequences." In this vacuum of understanding, what is a human being to do? We have no choice but to act, but in our actions we must cultivate the values that at least can best put us in a position for the best possible outcomes. Moore explains:

Man is responsible morally if not physically for any consequences of his acts, thoughts, or mere existence, even though frequently he cannot know or guess these consequences. Warren also believes in the freedom of the will, that man must live in an agony of choice. He is free to choose even though he cannot know the outcome of his choice and even though his choice may make little or no difference in the physical world; indeed, the result may be exactly the opposite of what he intended, although the more knowledge he has the less idealistic he is and the less history can surprise him. . . . Virtue, direction, meaning, values, significance are man's responsibility and do not reside in history itself. Man is a part of history and nature, but, Warren argues, if this is all he is, he is a nothing, a moral failure.

Jack Burden develops the theory of "the moral neutrality of history," which Moore defines: "History itself has no inherent values. . . . [It is] man's responsibility to make sense out of history." For Moore, this means that "the ultimate moral meaning of the cosmic web depends upon man, not history"; "man must remain ignorant of the consequences of even his most simple acts; hence his proper attitude is one of humility."[14]

We have no choice but to act. But we cannot know or control the outcomes of our actions. We cannot even know which actions are causes or to what extent they are causes or what effects our actions might have. Yet we must act. This is the "agony of choice" that Moore refers to. With the knowledge that our own actions function as causes in ways that lie beyond our own comprehension—with the understanding that we can shoot the arrow but that once we release it, we are powerless to control all the variables that determine where it will strike—we must, at the very least, act with an attitude of humility. Humility is the solution to the conundrum of the "agony of choice." This is what Jack means when he concludes the novel ready to reenter politics, but this time in service to a more ethically oriented government official, Hugh Miller, and also ready to reengage in his relationship with Anne, now releasing his idealized image of her and instead being ready, with her, to accept "the awful responsibility of Time."[15]

# 10

# Putting Humpty Dumpty Back Together

## "A Felt Need Will Be Satisfied"

About two and a half months after publishing *All the King's Men* (on August 17, 1946), Warren published the short story "Blackberry Winter" (on November 1). Although he was not as dedicated to the writing of short stories as he was to being a poet and novelist, this beautifully constructed story has always been highly praised and possibly one of the most anthologized of Warren's works. The narrator, an adult, looks back on his childhood to the day after a summer storm caused the creek to flood and there were dead farm animals (most notably chicks) floating in the water. The boy's father hires a vagrant looking for odd jobs to assist with the cleanup for the day. The story is a meditation on time, change, growing up, loss of innocence, and new awareness of the cycle of life. When the father has no further work to offer, the man responds with a word that shocks the boy and provokes the father to order the man to leave the farm immediately. The boy follows the man, who turns viciously to demand that he stop following. "But I did follow him," the man who was the boy tells us, "all the years."[1] Metaphorically, the boy, growing up, has in some way left his father to follow the stranger who disrupted their home that day. How has the narrator followed that man? By emulating his behavior? Or perhaps he has followed him only imaginatively? We are not told.

We are also not told that shocking word; the text of the story is silent on that detail. The omission is perhaps for the better because it leaves space for the reader's imagination. A specific word that might have been considered highly obscene in the 1940s (if it had even been approved for publication) could by now have lost its power to shock. That word, whatever it was, holds significance because it makes the entire story turn on language. The challenge to the father's authority, which the boy witnesses, is centered in language. The boy's temptation to travel into the realm of the transgressive, as represented by this mysterious stranger, is centered in language. The word, the use of language, has the power to subvert, overturn, disrupt, tempt, and seduce. The same can be said of Jack Burden, who literally disrupts his relationship with his father to follow a stranger, a father figure, who knows how to use words. Thus, "Blackberry Winter" has something in common with *All the King's Men*. Both narratives, produced in the same year, demonstrate the magnetic power of language as a tool of seduction.

Earlier in this study, I posed several interrelated questions: *How are the issues that Warren wrote about seventy years ago relevant to Americans today? Can we apply the lessons of Warren's narrative to our current political atmosphere? In what way can* All the King's Men *be an anchor for us now? What does* All the King's Men *tell us about power and ethics at this particular time in the history of Kentucky or the United States? Is this novel timeless and significant?* We have explored how the novel addresses these questions. We have surveyed answers offered by critics, journalists, and readers of the novel. I would like to offer some final considerations that ultimately return us to the power of political language.

In the survey of newspaper articles in chapter 3, we saw that political journalists working for differently oriented newspapers, Dwight Garner for the *New York Times* and Terry Teachout for the *Wall Street Journal,* have characterized the novel as "prescient" of the current political climate in our nation. I agree with their assessments. But as we have also seen, if Warren's narrative has achieved relevance to present-day circumstances, it is not because he had any special ability to foretell the future; it is because he told a story whose timelessness gives it renewed applications. As Justice Bill Cunningham says, "The book will remain relevant as long as we have representative government of elective officeholders."

The character Willie Stark, as we have seen, was based on the real-life politician Huey Long but is not merely Huey Long. He is any political player who compromises means and ends. He is every demagogue who manipulates language and manufactures an image of himself to seduce supporters. He is every politician who identifies a vacuum in the lives of his followers, which he fills with validation of their hopes and values. He is every politician who has a vacuum within himself, which he fills with the adulation of those followers.

As Mark Neikirk notes, "The times change; the nature of man doesn't." Though set in a particular time, as all narratives must be, the words and decisions and actions of its characters belong to the nature of humanity, which is not contained within any one year or decade or generation. Judge Sara Combs was on target in calling *All the King's Men* "a tale for all seasons of politics."

In a foundational work titled *The American Vision of Robert Penn Warren,* William Bedford Clark identifies "an implicit 'prophetic' strain present in Warren's work from the outset." This is not to say that Warren follows the model of a biblical prophet or even a

modern prophet calling for restoration of the past. Explaining Warren's use of the past, Clark says, "History, read honestly, offers us no
model for a Golden Age," and thus "to seek to renew in some pris-
tine sense the flawed covenant of the Founders is an exercise in use-
less sentimentality. But neither would it be wise, Warren insists, to
renounce their dream out of hand." The need that Warren identifies,
Clark explains, is neither renewal of the past nor repudiation of the
past but rather a "renegotiating of the covenant on pragmatic, but far
from unprincipled, terms."[2] Warren's depictions of Adam Stanton
and Willie Stark illustrate the dangers inherent in either extreme:
principle without pragmatism or pragmatism without principle.

The term *prophecy* or *prescience* is commonly understood to
mean "predictive" or "having foreknowledge of future events." This
definition limits what such texts are doing. Prophets are readers
and critics of their present circumstances. They are able to sound
notes of warning or hope for the future because they have the ability to read the present. Understood this way, dystopian novels such
as George Orwell's *1984,* Margaret Atwood's *The Handmaid's Tale,*
and Suzanne Collins's *Hunger Games* should be read not as their
authors' flights of fantasy but more productively as indictments of
current sociopolitical circumstances. They are works of cultural criticism. Accordingly, rather than *prophecy* or *prescience,* I prefer William Bedford Clark's term *vision* because Warren was visionary,
which is to say that he was a scrupulous and perceptive observer of
the Louisiana, United States, and Europe of the 1930s and 1940s as
well as a realistic but hopeful critic of human nature. Directed to
the present, the novelist's observations are criticisms. Directed to the
future, those observations may be taken as warnings. Future readers
hold the prerogative to determine the novel's areas of ongoing relevance and application.

Warren's criticisms or warnings are depicted in the narrative,
as we have seen: the rhetoric of the populist demagogue (the seducer

who "could talk so good), the pandering speaker (who roils emotions and avoids any attempt "to improve their minds"), the self-centered elected official who dictates that aides and the media should serve his interests rather than the public's ("Who do I work for?"). I believe that the most significant warnings from the novel—the dangers most relevant to our political culture today—reside within the depictions of Willie Stark as a manipulator of rhetoric to fulfill people's needs. This is where demagogues are most seductive. But this is also where the novel offers hope because it calls upon all of us as citizens to hold ourselves accountable for the support and votes that we freely choose to give.

In Frank Gado's interview of Warren in 1966, Warren spoke about a vacuum (here with reference to the dramatic script of *All the King's Men*). These comments from the author are highly significant for us: "The notion—or *a* notion—behind the play was that a man gains power because he is drawn into a vacuum of power. In one sense, [that man] is a creation of history. . . . The narrator, Burden, has a 'vacuum'—purposelessness—that Stark can fill. The bodyguard stutters, and Stark 'talks so good.' And so on with the mistress and others. For each individual, the 'strong man' is a fulfillment. Here the individuals are the mirrors to society, in a sense."[3]

Warren explained that he needed a context for Stark: "Power moving into a vacuum. So I got my vacuum fellow, or, as it were, my partial vacuum fellow, into the story. . . . The newspaperman helps illustrate it." Warren continued with a description of Jack that is not flattering: Jack has "a grave defect of character and personality—and he knows it. He's blind in certain ways and he's ready to be a tool, to enter someone else's magnetic field. Sounds awful, doesn't it? But it's a constant thing—power operates that way."[4]

What characterizes the vacuum within each voter? Warren addressed that question in the interview as well. Each of us, he said, has "a natural need to build something, to be part of a cause, to gain meaning." Of course, such needs can and do attract us to commit ourselves to productive projects. We organize ourselves into businesses and civic organizations, religious communities and nonprofits. We innovate and create, volunteer to help others, and join the neighborhood cleanup. But Warren pointed out that this need to be part of a cause "can get to be an evil thing when the great blankness of life is filled by terrible forces. Look at what happens when this sense of cause is stimulated by a Hitler or Mussolini."[5]

Warren's use of the terms *vacuum fellow* and *tool* designate Jack Burden as a device in the narrative. We could apply that designation further to refer to *vacuum characters,* all of those such as Sadie Burke and Sugar-Boy and the nameless members of the cheering crowds who enter the *magnetic field* of Willie Stark and function as vacuums for the rhetoric that Willie offers. Then we must apply these terms to ourselves. Willie is the *magnetic character.* We must examine how we function as *vacuum characters* for any candidates we support and vote for. *All the King's Men* challenges us to examine our political landscape to identify anyone who creates a magnetic field that draws in followers. We must be aware of vacuums that exist in today's politics and of the political actors who are attempting to move into those vacuums to take power.

Warren noted in the interview that the vacuums we create for demagogues to exploit are not only personal but also governmental. When he was living in Louisiana, he wondered how Huey Long was able to grab power like a strong man. "It didn't happen out of the blue," he says, "There had to be a context beforehand." That context is depicted, as we have seen, when the *Chronicle* sends Jack Burden to cover Willie Stark's campaign. The newspaper has been uncovering corruption throughout the state, with Mason City being the example in the argument for reform. "When you have incompetent or bad government long enough," Warren stated, "you get Willie Stark. Somebody had to move in to fill the vacuum. It doesn't have to be a vacuum of power; it can be thought of as a vacuum of social goods. A felt need will be satisfied, one way or other, and it doesn't matter whether Stark is just making promises or is actually trying to deliver on them."[6] We should notice here Warren's phrasing: people need to feel that their needs are being addressed, so they will support the candidates who promise to address those needs, regardless of whether those promises are kept. That is a context for demagoguery. So, again, considering the relevance of this novel today, we are compelled to be mindful of how our current city, state, and federal governments function or malfunction in ways that create openings for demagogues to promise reform. As *All the King's Men* demonstrates, "a felt need will be satisfied."

Finally, we must not overlook the hope that Warren's vision offers. The support and the votes that we citizens possess belong to us; they are ours to give or withhold freely. We must hold leaders accountable, of course, but we must also hold ourselves accountable. Each of us can do this by being mindful of our own needs and our own vulnerabilities to political candidates who appeal to those needs. We must be watchful of potential authoritarians who seem more committed to the public's adulation than to service to the public. We must maintain awareness of how each of us fills the role of "follower."

*All the King's Men* demonstrates how a populist demagogue can use language to manipulate other people to his advantage. Therefore, we must seek politicians who do try to "improve [our] minds," who challenge us to consider new information, and who ask us to think critically rather than merely trying to make us feel good with inspiring orations. To make this happen, we absolutely must learn and understand how rhetoric works to persuade us. Students must be able to identify the techniques that candidates and elected officials may use. American middle schools, high schools, and universities must teach the techniques of rhetoric and persuasion in English, language arts, reading, and speech courses. Courses in history and political science can demonstrate how those techniques have been employed historically to persuade citizens in every context from political campaigns to military actions.

The Common Core State Standards and Kentucky Core Academic Standards already include a broad spectrum of expectations for students to engage not only in the literary analysis of poetry, drama, and fiction but also in the close reading and rhetorical analysis of informational texts. Whatever changes are made to those initiatives, parents and all citizens should demand that school curricula retain those standards for students to achieve mastery of rhetorical analysis. As a dedicated teacher and textbook author in the disciplines of literature, writing, and rhetoric, Robert Penn Warren would agree, I believe, that education in language and in all of the humanities remains the greatest instrument to ensure the continuing health of democracy and the progress of liberty in this great experiment known as the United States of America. As a political tale for all seasons, *All the King's Men* is a tale of caution for all generations, but it is also a tale of hope for America's future.

# "To Love So Well the World"

## Remembering Robert Penn Warren

June 12, 2010. A rainy Saturday morning. Cheryl and I have begun the first day of our trip to literary sites in the Hudson River Valley. From Albany, we take Highway 7, crossing the border into Vermont, passing a store that sells souvenirs and real maple syrup. We drive past Bennington and Old Bennington, where we stop to visit Robert Frost's house, stand in the very room where he wrote "Stopping by Woods," and look out the window at the state highway that adjoined the property even in Frost's day.

We're feeling the anticipation that all travelers feel who are about to engage with something yet who also seek disengagement from time, far away from the world of campaigns and sound bites, dirt and deals. We have disconnected in order to reconnect.

We continue into Green Mountain National Forest. No turn-off is noted on the Google map we're using, so we try one road (which turns out to be a driveway). Farther up we discover that we seem to be going too far, so we double back and see an overpass. We take the exit going west, the opposite way of where we want to go, figuring that we can reverse our direction over the overpass and head east. That takes us on the correct path—toward Stratton, Vermont.

At Exit 3, we take South Road north and then turn right at Kansas Road, which brings us eastward across the overpass. Kansas Road turns into Kelley Stand Road. Kelley twists, turns, and curves so much that we are going north, south, east, and sometimes seemingly a combination of all directions. We can see on the map that it will be a dirt road, but there's no dirt yet. We ask a local person who is jogging. He says a dirt road is up the way we are going, but he warns that it's rough going, and he advises us to turn back and go up Highway 7 to the next exit, then go to West Wardsboro (which is east of Stratton), then drive from there to Stratton. That sounds complicated. Consulting the map, we realize that his route would be a long circular way of getting to Stratton, so we decide to press onward.

Driving farther, we still wonder when the dirt road will appear. We ask another local person who is walking her dogs. She tells us that we passed the dirt road and should have turned right at a fork a way back. Now we realize we are driving on roads not on the map. As we drive away, we remark to each other that we hope we can ask some more locals for directions because we enjoy hearing their beautiful, distinctive Vermont accents.

A large creek runs alongside the road, filled with boulders, campers visible at various points along the banks. At one point, we lose the creek but rejoin it later when Kelley Stand Road turns into Stratton Arlington Road. Now the road is dirt all the way, but fortunately it has been graded recently, so the ride is not too bumpy. "Enter at your own risk" kinds of signs appear at various points to warn drivers that the road is not tended during the winter months.

The scenery is lush, with the creek on our right and a steep incline of mountain on our left. Rocks and trees on our left lean threateningly toward the road as if they are ready to take the leap or the fall into the roadway at any time.

Finally, after driving at great length along Stratton Arlington Road, we arrive in Stratton. The town seems little more than a crossroad in the midst of the woods.

We have no idea where the cemetery might be located. Pausing at the crossroad, we are uncertain of whether to continue forward or turn left. A small wooden town building is visible at the crossroad. We stop to ask directions, but the building is closed. Cheryl has the phone number of the town clerk, whom she had written to in advance. We try to call but cannot get a signal on our cell phones. So we decide to continue in the straight-ahead direction. We pass various small roads that lead to farmhouses. At times, we must make guesses about whether to take a left or right whenever a road forks. But the trick, we discover, is to stay straight on the same road.

We eventually find ourselves at Willis Cemetery Road. We continue along the gravel-dirt road—a little bumpy. We arrive at another fork, with Willis Cemetery Road continuing to the right. We take that right and keep going until we cannot go any farther— the literal end of the road. We stop, park, turn off the engine. After all the driving and the mental noise of getting lost, the silence is palpable. Trees and brush tower high all around us. To our right, through some trees, we see grave stones, a cemetery. In the light rain, we walk on the soggy ground through the trees. We emerge into a small clearing, home to approximately forty scattered graves, bordered by four waist-high, dry-masonry stone walls. Beyond those walls are the surrounding woods, holding the whole scene in an embrace. We have arrived. Willis Cemetery. Two large slabs toward the back:

ROBERT PENN WARREN
Born Guthrie, Kentucky
Apr. 24, 1905
Died Stratton
Sept. 15, 1989

ELEANOR CLARK WARREN
Born Los Angeles, CA.
July 6, 1913
Died Boston, MA.
Feb. 16, 1996

I remove the photocopied pages from my pocket and hand Cheryl's paper to her. Each of us is grasping an umbrella with one hand while protecting the dry paper in the other hand. Standing at the graves, we read aloud.

Cheryl begins. She recites "Evening Hawk." The poem's narrator gazes upward to his aspirations and inward to his daily experience. The gliding hawk is the poet's metaphor for the larger context of history:

His wing
Scythes down another day, his motion
Is that of the honed steel-edge, we hear
The crashless fall of stalks of time.[1]

It's my turn. The poem that I have selected is "Masts at Dawn," a poem I have read many times over the years. The final lines conclude with an inversion of John 3:16. The speaker yearns for meaning and searches for a way to act in this world:

I lie in my bed and think how, in darkness, the masts go white.

The sound of the engine of the first fishing dory dies seaward.
Soon
In the inland glen wakes the dawn-dove. We must try
To love so well the world that we may believe, in the end, in
   God.[2]

As raindrops lightly tap the umbrellas above us, we place Mr. Warren's poems at the base of his gravestone. The awkward moment
every traveler knows has arrived—the moment when we realize that
the experience has come to an end, the moment of turning away
from the monument or the battlefield or the historical marker that
until now had been the implacable knowledge of the travel book,
the itinerary, and the map but that henceforward will be the pliable
knowledge of memory.

   After a final backward glance at the gravesite through the rain,
we return to the rental car and then to New York and ultimately
back to Kentucky.

# Acknowledgments

This project was supported in part by a Professional Development Award from the Northern Kentucky University College of Arts and Sciences.

I wish to thank the following individuals:

Leila W. Salisbury, director, University Press of Kentucky, for developing the idea for this project, inviting me to write the book, and guiding me in the process

Diana McGill, dean of the College of Arts and Sciences at Northern Kentucky University (NKU), for her support

Mark Neikirk, director of the Scripps Howard Center for Civic Engagement at NKU, for his support, advice, and assistance in making contacts with individuals in Kentucky journalism and for the insights he shared with me in our conversations about *All the King's Men*

Adam Caswell, assistant vice president for government, corporate, and foundation engagement at NKU, for assisting me in making contacts with elected and appointed officials in Kentucky government

Jill Liebisch, graduate research assistant at W. Frank Steely Library at NKU, for assisting me in making the search for news sources more efficient

Robert Zai, associate dean of the library and Jill Liebisch's faculty mentor at NKU, for his consultation

Anita Southwick, manager of Research Compliance, Office of Research, Grants, and Contracts, NKU, for assistance in the IRB process

Jessica Chiccehitto Hindman, my colleague in the NKU English Department, writer and teacher of creative nonfiction, for reading and responding to a section of the manuscript

John Alberti and Emily Detmer-Goebel, current and past chairs of the NKU Department of English, for their encouragement

Cheryl L. Cullick, for her reading of the manuscript, her advice on matters of substance and editing, and her support

I invited seventy officials in all three branches of Kentucky government and in balanced numbers across political parties, including officeholders at the highest levels, to contribute their experiences and thoughts about *All the King's Men*. My request was certainly an imposition, given that some might not have read the novel for a long time or even not at all. The following individuals in elected offices and appointed positions in Kentucky state government and in Kentucky journalism responded to my invitation to contribute to this project. I thank them all.

Steve Beshear, former governor of the Commonwealth of Kentucky

Justice Bill Cunningham of the Kentucky Supreme Court

Judge Sara Combs of the Kentucky Court of Appeals

Michael Benson, president of Eastern Kentucky University

Geoffrey Mearns, former president of NKU and former federal prosecutor in the US Department of Justice

Gary Ransdell, president of Western Kentucky University (home of the Robert Penn Warren Collection)

Aaron Thompson, president of Kentucky State University

Bill Goodman, executive director of the Kentucky Humanities Council and host and managing editor of the public-affairs series *Kentucky Tonight* on Kentucky Educational Television

Al Cross, contributing political columnist for the *Louisville Courier-Journal* and director of the Institute for Rural Journalism and Community Issues at the University of Kentucky

Tom Eblen, metro/state columnist and former managing editor for the *Lexington Herald-Leader*

David Hawpe, former editor of the *Louisville Courier-Journal* and current senior aide to Kentucky State senator Morgan McGarvey and member of the University of Kentucky Board of Trustees

Jamie Lucke, editorial writer for the *Lexington Herald-Leader*

Mark Neikirk, former editor of the *Kentucky Post* and director of the Scripps-Howard Center for Civic Engagement at NKU

Finally, I wish to express my enduring gratitude to two of my past teachers, without whom this project would not exist: Dr. Peter Stitt introduced me to Warren's work when I was an undergraduate student and Dr. Steven Weisenburger mentored my study of Warren in graduate school at the University of Kentucky. Their work is testimony to the truism that a teacher's influence is unbound by time.

*Appendix*

# Questions for Discussion

The questions given here invite the reader to consider the relevance of *All the King's Men* to the contemporary political atmosphere in the United States.

1. Mark Neikirk, director of the Scripps Howard Center for Civic Engagement and former editor of the *Kentucky Post,* offers a memory of the joys of reading *All the King's Men* in his youth: "It was an inside tour of politics, along with a nice coming-of-age romance thing that resonated, too, including the betrayal part—[taken] at an age when one's heart get broken and love, like politics, gets a reality check and takes a step back from blind idealism." How does *All the King's Men* give politics a "reality check"? How does Jack Burden's friendship with Adam Stanton and his on–off relationship with Anne Stanton reflect themes in the political plot?

2. Gary Ransdell, president of Western Kentucky University, writes that *All the King's Men* "is particularly important reading for those who might be pondering a career in politics." Similarly, Steve Beshear, former governor of Kentucky, states, "The book's practi-

cal value is that it asks two important questions: Why does one seek elected office, and should you win that office, how are you going to govern?" Consider how *All the King's Men* could be part of the preparation of a young person who is deciding on a career in politics. What might this novel offer him or her? What can he or she learn from it regarding how to govern?

3. David Hawpe, former editor of the *Louisville Courier-Journal*, identifies *All the King's Men* as "one of the books people should read in order to understand America's political values and civic culture, which lionizes the self-made individual, resists the strictures of government, and celebrates winning as a self-sufficient good." Would you agree? What exactly are America's political values, and how would you characterize America's civic culture? What can the novel add to someone's understanding of those values and culture?

4. Judge Sara Combs of the Kentucky Court of Appeals says of *All the King's Men,* "It is the saga essentially of every dictator who has risen from populist roots to realize his dreams of empire. It crosses geographic borders and transcends social classes—from Lenin to Willie Stark to . . . ? We continue to provide nominees to carry on the series." What names, in the United States or in the world, would you add to that series?

5. Justice Bill Cunningham of the Kentucky Supreme Court considers the usefulness of *All the King's Men* for students. "The story of Jack Burden and Willie Stark has led me to ask many youngsters this solid question about democracy: 'Had you rather had an ineffective leader or a corrupt one?'" How would you respond to his question?

6. Bill Goodman, director of the Kentucky Humanities Council, says, "An argument could be made in today's political climate

that the novel resonates with themes present in the nation's mood; the common person, working-class whites, and political posturing seem to be playing out today just as [they] did seventy years ago. The deceitful shenanigans of yesterday might prove to be good study for power-hungry politicians of today." How would you characterize today's national mood? Does the novel reflect that mood in some way? Are characters, elements of the plot, or themes from the novel being played out today?

7. Al Cross, contributing political columnist for the *Louisville Courier-Journal* and director of the Institute for Rural Journalism and Community Issues at the University of Kentucky, asks, "What lessons can government officials and citizens learn from the book?" Cross provides his own answer. What would be your answer to his question?

8. For David Hawpe, *All the King's Men* is a cautionary tale, one that anticipated the rise of future Willie Starks long after its publication in 1946. "It's almost too obvious that *All the King's Men* anticipates the incendiary populism of today's national politics," says Hawpe. What connections would you make between the novel's depiction of politics and the politics of today or the recent past? Do you see any current uses of the terms *populist* or *demagogue* that align with Willie Stark or that, upon closer comparison, are really different from their application to Willie Stark?

9. Tom Eblen, metro/state columnist for and former managing editor of the *Lexington Herald-Leader,* discusses passages that have affected him because of their beauty or power. He states, "Descriptive prose doesn't get any better than this." What is one passage in *All the King's Men* that you especially enjoyed—a passage that amazed you or surprised you—because of its beauty and power?

What specific words or phrasings made that passage stand out to you, and why?

10. Robert Penn Warren stated in an interview by Frank Gado in 1966 that powerful leaders or potential demagogues move into vacuums that exist in government and in the lives of their individual followers. Those demagogues are like magnets that attract followers to them. What circumstances in government might create the risk of a vacuum that a demagogue could take advantage of? What qualities in a powerful leader work like a magnet to attract the support of citizens?

11. In a well-known passage in chapter 1 of *All the King's Men,* Willie Stark explains his philosophy of using negative information—what he calls "dirt"—to force positive results. Re-read that passage in your copy of the novel. Is Willie Stark's assessment of "dirt" correct? Is it useful? What are the potential consequences of government officials' adoption of this philosophy?

12. Willie Stark articulates his belief that all humanity is corrupt. Therefore, the good can never be created per se; it must always be created out of the bad. When Adam asks how to distinguish good from bad, Stark replies that it depends on circumstance and individual preference. Re-read that passage in chapter 6 of your copy of the novel. Is Willie Stark's philosophy of goodness correct or usable? What are the potential consequences of the adoption of this philosophy by people who hold elected office?

# Notes

## Preface

1. Robert Penn Warren, *All the King's Men* (New York: Harcourt Brace, 1946), 421, 72. All quotations from the novel come from this edition.

## Introduction

1. Kentucky Arts Council, "Kentucky Writers' Day," n.d., at http://artscouncil.ky.gov/KAC/Showcasing/Event_WritersDay.htm, accessed August 11, 2017.

2. Kentucky Historical Society, Historical Marker Database, n.d., at http://migration.kentucky.gov/kyhs/hmdb/MarkerSearch.aspx?mode=County&county=110, accessed August 11, 2017; Guthrie, Kentucky, "About," n.d., at http://guthrieky.com/about-2/, accessed August 11, 2017; Robert Penn Warren Birthplace Museum, website, n.d., at https://www.robertpennwarren.com/birthpla.html, accessed August 11, 2017; "Author Robert Penn Warren Honored on US. Postage Stamp," PR Newswire, April 4, 2005, at http://www.prnewswire.com/news-releases/author-robert-penn-warren-honored-on-us-postage-stamp-54169642.html.

3. Robert Penn Warren, "The World of Daniel Boone," *Holiday,* December 1963.

4. Robert Penn Warren, *Brother to Dragons* (1953; reprint, Baton Rouge: Louisiana State University Press, 1979), xiii.

5. Jonathan Gottschall, *The Storytelling Animal: How Stories Make Us Human* (Boston: Mariner Books, 2013).

6. Daniel Wattenberg, "The Lady Macbeth of Little Rock," *American Spectator,* November 20, 2015, at https://spectator.org/64729_lady-macbeth-little-rock/; Jonathan Freedland, "Enough of Playing Hamlet: Obama Needs to Act Now," *Guardian,* September 3, 2013, at https://www.theguardian.com/commentisfree/2013/sep/03/enough-hamlet-obama-act-now-syria.

7. Melissa Block (host) and Ron Elving, "Willie Stark Lives On," *All Things Considered,* National Public Radio, September 8, 2008, at http://www.npr.org/templates/story/story.php?storyId=94394578.

8. Robert Penn Warren, *Audubon: A Vision,* in *The Collected Poems of Robert Penn Warren,* edited by John Burt (Baton Rouge: Louisiana State University Press, 1998), 267.

## 1. The Life of Robert Penn Warren

1. For information about Warren's life and work, see Joseph Blotner, *Robert Penn Warren: A Biography* (New York: Random House, 1997); Robert Penn Warren Circle, website, n.d., at http://www.robertpennwarren .com/, accessed August 11, 2017; Center for Robert Penn Warren Studies, Western Kentucky University, website, n.d., at https://www.wku.edu/rpw/, accessed August 11, 2017; Robert Penn Warren Center and Library, Western Kentucky University, website, n.d., at https://www.wku.edu/rpw/ and https://www.wku. edu/library/dlsc/kentucky-library/rpwlib.php, accessed August 11, 2017.

2. Robert Penn Warren, "An Interview with Robert Penn Warren," interview by Peter Stitt, in *Conversations with Robert Penn Warren,* ed. Gloria L. Cronin and Ben Siegel (Jackson: University Press of Mississippi, 2005), 122.

3. Robert Penn Warren to Frank Lawrence Owsley, January 31, 1950, in Robert Penn Warren, *Selected Letters of Robert Penn Warren,* vol. 3: *Triumph and Transition, 1943–1952,* ed. Randy Hendricks and James A. Perkins (Baton Rouge: Louisiana State University Press, 2006), 353.

4. Warren, *Audubon,* 266.

## 2. An Overview of *All the King's Men*

1. Robert Penn Warren to Lambert Davis, editor at Harcourt Brace, January 28, 1943, and to Allen Tate, January 31, 1944, in *Selected Letters of Robert Penn Warren,* 3:11, 60.

2. Warren, *All the King's Men,* 49; see Psalm 51:5, "Behold, I was brought forth in iniquity, and in sin did my mother conceive me" (Revised Standard Version).

3. Harold Woodell, All the King's Men: *The Search for a Usable Past,* Twayne Masterwork Studies no. 112 (New York: Twayne, 1993), 13, 15.

4. Blotner, *Robert Penn Warren,* 220, 229.

5. Robert McCrum, "The 100 Best Novels: No. 67—*All the King's Men* by Robert Penn Warren (1946)," *Guardian,* December 29, 2014, https://www.the-guardian.com/books/series/the-100-best-novels?page=2; "100 Best Novels," Modern Library, n.d., at http://www.modernlibrary.com/top-100/100-best-novels/, accessed August 11, 2017.

## 3. *All the King's Men* in Political and Popular Culture

1. Chuck Sweeny, "Defiant Blagojevich Proves That Power Is the Ultimate Drug," *Rockford Register Star,* December 28, 2008, at http://www.rrstar.com/article/20081228/News/312289960; Cheryl Truman, "Governor Alone Is Cause for Federal Aid," *Lexington Herald-Leader,* June 20, 2003; "Broader Consequences"

(editorial), *Frankfort State Journal,* January 28, 2003; Adam Kirsch, "Willie Stark, the un-Obama, and Idealism's Limits," *Toronto Star,* September 22, 2012.

2. Michael Washburn, "At 70, *All the King's Men* Is the Book for This Campaign Season," WFPL radio, November 7, 2016, at http://wfpl.org/all-kings-men-book-campaign-season-2016/; Carter Eskew, "Is Obama Supporting Clinton or Sanders?" *Washington Post,* January 29, 2016.

3. Jonah Goldberg, "Trump and Sanders Break the Mold for Populist Politicians," *National Review,* December 30, 2015, at http://www.nationalreview.com/article/429087/donald-trump-bernie-sanderss-populist-politics?target=author&tid=897; Dwight Garner, "70 Years On, It's Politics as Unusual," *New York Times,* April 12, 2016, at https://www.nytimes.com/2016/04/12/books/all-the-kings-men-now70-has-a-touch-of-2016.html; Terry Teachout, "The Prescience of a Political Novel," *Wall Street Journal,* March 24, 2016; Mark Caleb Smith, "All of Trump's Men: This Race Is Starting to Remind Us of a Novel," *Dayton Daily News,* April 2, 2016, at http://www.mydaytondailynews.com/news/opinion/all-trump-men-this-race-starting-remind-novel/OwccmGIhxsRzRG47PQ1FbO/.

4. Carl Bernstein and Bob Woodward, *All the President's Men* (New York: Simon and Schuster, 1974); William Bedford Clark, "From *All the King's Men* to *Primary Colors,*" *America,* December 28, 1996, 26; Robert Penn Warren, "A Conversation with Robert Penn Warren," interview by Bill Moyers, WNET television, April 4, 1976, in *Conversations with Robert Penn Warren,* ed. Cronin and Siegel, 93–94.

5. Anonymous [Joe Klein], *Primary Colors: A Novel of Politics* (New York: Random House, 1996).

6. Robert Penn Warren to Frank Lawrence Owsley, May 11, 1949, in *Selected Letters of Robert Penn Warren,* 3:339.

7. Robert Penn Warren, "Robert Penn Warren: Willie Stark, Politics, and the Novel," interview by William Kennedy (1973), in *Conversations with Robert Penn Warren,* ed. Cronin and Siegel, 89.

8. A survey of reviews of the 2006 film demonstrate these and other criticisms across the board in national and local newspapers. However, a good place to start would be the reviews by A. O. Scott in the *New York Times* (September 22, 2006), Todd McCarthy in *Variety* (September 10, 2006), and Ty Burr in the *Boston Globe* (September 22, 2006).

9. Robert Penn Warren, *All the King's Men* (script) (New York: Samuel French, n.d.), http://www.samuelfrench.com/p/12949/all-the-kings-men-warren, accessed August 11, 2017; Robert Penn Warren, *All the King's Men* (play), in *Robert Penn Warren's* All the King's Men: *Three Stage Versions,* ed. James A. Grimshaw Jr. and James A. Perkins (Athens: University of Georgia Press, 2000), 175. The Samuel French webpage for ordering the script lists these snippets from reviews: "Willie in all his personal relationships is a fascinating man and often a winning man, too. . . . What is right and what is wrong? Mr. Warren makes a stimulating inquiry into that troublesome question" (*New York Times*); "*All the King's Men*

went off with a roof-shaking bang. . . . This is the most engrossing drama seen off Broadway in months" (*New York World Telegram & Sun*); "This drama by Robert Penn Warren is a blockbuster. It is a major Off-Broadway event. . . . A subtle and rich study of man in society" (*Cue Magazine*). See Robert Penn Warren to Leonard Casper, September 28, 1959; Allen Tate, October 28, 1959; and William Bandy, October 26, 1959, in *Selected Letters of Robert Penn Warren*, vol. 4: *New Beginnings and New Directions, 1953–1968*, ed. Randy Henricks and James A. Perkins (Baton Rouge: Louisiana State University Press, 2008), 263–67.

10. Carlisle Floyd, score and libretto, *Willie Stark, the Opera*, staging by Harold Prince, Houston Grand Opera, PBS, aired in 1981, at https://vimeo.com/134655406.

11. Boosey & Hawkes, "Floyd, Carlisle: *Willie Stark* (1980)," n.d., at http://www.boosey.com/pages/opera/moredetails?musicid=6995, accessed August 11, 2017; John Duka, "*Willie Stark:* From Opera House to Home Screen," *New York Times*, September 27, 1981, at http://www.nytimes.com/1981/09/27/theater/willie-stark-from-opera-house-to-home-screen.html?pagewanted=all; John O'Connor, "Carlisle Floyd's *Willie Stark* on PBS," *New York Times*, September 28, 1981, at http://www.nytimes.com/1981/09/28/arts/tv-carlisle-floyd-s-willie-stark-on-pbs.html; Donal Henahan, "Floyd's *Willie*," *New York Times*, April 27, 1981, at http://www.nytimes.com/1981/04/27/arts/opera-floyd-s-willie.html. Warren himself expressed a bemused attitude toward the whole opera enterprise. In one letter, for example, he says, "Me and opera are indeed a joke. I go, but only because Eleanor is made for music. I guess I'll go to this one out of curiosity" (Robert Penn Warren to Charles H. Foster, 1980, in *Selected Letters of Robert Penn Warren*, vol. 6: *Toward Sunset, at a Great Height, 1980–1989*, ed. Randy Hendricks and James A. Perkins [Baton Rouge: Louisiana State University Press, 2013], 21).

## 4. The Timelessness of *All the King's Men*

1. Clark, "From *All the King's Men* to *Primary Colors*," 26; Sara Combs, email to author, May 12, 2017.

2. Robert Penn Warren, "A Note to *All the King's Men*," *Sewanee Review* 61 (1953): 479–80, and "Introduction to the Modern Library Edition," in *A Robert Penn Warren Reader* (New York: Vintage Books, 1987), 227–28.

3. For comparisons of Huey Long and Willie Stark, see Hamilton Basso, "The Huey Long Legend," *Life*, December 9, 1946; Ken Burns, *Huey Long*, documentary, PBS, September 28, 1985, at http://www.pbs.org/kenburns/hueylong/; Ladell Payne, "Willie Stark and Huey Long: Atmosphere, Myth, or Suggestion?" *American Quarterly* 20 (1968): 580–95, reprinted in *Robert Penn Warren: Critical Perspectives*, ed. Neil Nakadate (Lexington: University Press of Kentucky, 1981), 77–92.

4. Robert Penn Warren to Lambert Davis, editor at Harcourt Brace, January 28, 1943, in *Selected Letters of Robert Penn Warren*, 3:10. Incidentally, in another letter the following year, Warren again referred to the novel as a political novel:

"At present I'm in the middle of a new book—a novel about Southern politics, if its 'aboutness' can be described in that way" (Robert Penn Warren to Malcolm Cowley, April 8, 1944, in *Selected Letters of Robert Penn Warren,* 3:67).

5. Warren, "A Note to *All the King's Men,*" 480; Warren, "Introduction to the Modern Library Edition," 228; Warren, quoted in Burns, *Huey Long.*

6. Robert Penn Warren, "A Conversation with Robert Penn Warren," interview by Frank Gado, February 8, 1966, in *Talking with Robert Penn Warren,* ed. Floyd Watkins, John Hiers, and Mary Louise Weaks (Athens: University of Georgia Press, 1990), 69. It is notable that Warren refers to his novel here as a "political novel." Similarly, when he had questions about politics during the revision process for *All the King's Men,* he turned to Brainard "Lon" Cheney, a friend of his since Vanderbilt University. Cheney served on the staff of US senator from Tennessee Tom Steward and as public-relations director for Tennessee governor Frank Clement. See *Selected Letters of Robert Penn Warren,* 4:11 n. 7.

7. Joyce Carol Oates, "*All the King's Men*—a Case of Misreading?" review of the restored edition of *All the King's Men* edited by Noel Polk, *New York Review of Books,* March 28, 2002, at http://www.nybooks.com/articles/2002/03/28/all-the-kings-mena-case-of-misreading/.

8. Robert Penn Warren, "*All the King's Men:* The Matrix of Experience," *Yale Review* 53 (1963): 161.

9. Ibid., 166–67.

10. Quoted in James A. Grimshaw Jr. and James A. Perkins, "Introduction," in *Robert Penn Warren's* All the King's Men, ed. Grimshaw and Perkins, 9.

11. Flannery O'Connor and Robert Penn Warren, "An Interview with Flannery O'Connor and Robert Penn Warren," in *Conversations with Robert Penn Warren,* ed. Cronin and Siegel, 27.

12. Block and Elving, "Willie Stark Lives On." Elving adds an interesting thought on the development of the character's name: "Warren in Italy wrote a verse drama about a man named Talus, an allusion to a mythic Greek hero. As he converted that poetry into the prose of the novel, he renamed his character Willie Talos. His editor hated that name, so Warren suggested Willie Strong, which sounded too much like Long. And they compromised on the German word for strong, Stark."

13. David Madden, interviewed in ibid.

14. Michael Benson, email to author, June 6, 2017.

15. Psychologist Martin E. P. Seligman and science writer John Tierney recently made the argument that "we aren't built to live in the present moment," which offers one explanation for the ways we apply memories, even memories of fictional characters, to future situations. "The brain's long-term memory has often been compared to an archive, but that's not its primary purpose. Instead of faithfully recording the past, it keeps rewriting history. Recalling an event in a new context can lead to new information being inserted in the memory." This rewriting of past events is not a defect in our memory; to the contrary, it is essential to the way we remember because "the point of memory is to improve our

ability to face the present and the future. To exploit the past, we metabolize it by extracting and recombining relevant information to fit novel situations." We think we understand a new experience when we situate it with reference to a previous story. We revise our understanding of that previous story with reference to the new experience. We do this with fictional characters as much as with real people from our collective histories ("We Aren't Built to Live in the Moment," *New York Times,* May 19, 2017, at https://www.nytimes.com/2017/05/19/opinion/sunday/why-the-future-is-always-on-your-mind.html?_r=0).

### 5. Impressions of *All the King's Men*

1. In this chapter, I quote the following respondents to the queries I sent out to political officeholders, university officials, and journalists: Michael Benson, email to the author, June 6, 2017; Steve Beshear, email to the author, April 26, 2017; Sara Combs, email to the author, May 12, 2017; Al Cross, email to the author, June 3, 2017; Bill Cunningham, email to the author, April 13, 2017; Tom Eblen, email to the author, May 31, 2017; Bill Goodman, email to the author, May 29, 2017; David Hawpe, email to the author, May 24, 2017; Jamie Lucke, email to the author, May 31, 2017; Geoffrey Mearns, interview by the author, Highland Heights, KY, April 14, 2017; Mark Neikirk, email to the author, April 19, 2017; Gary Ransdell, email to author, May 1, 2017; Aaron Thompson, email to the author, May 15, 2017.

2. Warren, *All the King's Men*, 1.

3. Oates, *"All the King's Men*—a Case of Misreading?"

4. Robert Penn Warren, *Portrait of a Father* (Lexington: University Press of Kentucky, 1988), 14.

5. To put Cross's comments in context, his survey of Kentucky politics is worth quoting at length here:

> Jimmy Carter, who promised to never lie to us, was elected partly as an antidote to that unhappiness and cynicism [of the Vietnam and Watergate era], but he, too, was a human being with flaws in personality and judgment, and we replaced him with a former movie actor who knew how to sell himself. In Kentucky, that election (Reagan carried the state by 1.5 percentage points) was the beginning of a historic turn to the Republican Party and the social conservatism that it increasingly adopted and that reflected the fundamental beliefs of our state, which is a whole 'nother story.
>
> But that turn relates to *All the King's Men* in this way: Kentucky was once less of an issues state than a patronage state, one in which a relatively poor electorate wanted things from the government, much like Willie Stark's state and Huey Long's Louisiana. Kentucky became more prosperous and more educated (those go hand in hand) but retained most of its social conservatism, and the issues driven by that ideology are now usually those that matter most. This conservatism runs deep and goes back to the presidential candidacy of a

Catholic (JFK lost the state by more than 7 percentage points), the Supreme Court ruling against official school prayer, the civil rights movement (more than a generation later, about 15 percent of Kentucky voters in exit polls acknowledged racial animus against Barack Obama), abortion, and gay rights.

Kentucky has also been a state that has been, like Stark's and Louisiana, too tolerant of official corruption. I believe this stems partly from our large number of small counties, where politics tend to be family—or clique—oriented and political office is often viewed as partly a private possession, not just a public trust. In much of rural Kentucky, voters expect local officials to help themselves and their allies, part of the logic being, "Why fool with all this trouble unless you can help yourself, your family, and your friends?" . . . The pay is better now, but the tradition of legal and illegal corruption lives on; one national survey of state-level journalists ranked Kentucky at or near the top in both forms of corruption.

## 6. How the Story Works

1. Simone Vauthier, "The Case of the Vanishing Narratee: An Inquiry into *All the King's Men*," *Southern Literary Journal* 6, no. 2 (Spring 1974): 42.

2. Warren, *All the King's Men*, 1.

3. Vauthier, "The Case of the Vanishing Narratee," 43.

4. David Hawpe, email to the author, May 24, 2017.

5. Tom Eblen, email to the author, May 31, 2017.

## 7. The Rhetoric of the Populist Demagogue

1. Warren, *All the King's Men*, 421.

2. Warren, *All the King's Men* (play), 179, 227.

3. The idea of political seduction—politics as a form of seduction—has been mentioned with some frequency in scholarship about *All the King's Men*. See, for example, Clark, *American Vision of Robert Penn Warren*, and Lucy Ferris, *Sleeping with the Boss: Female Subjectivity and Narrative Pattern in Robert Penn Warren* (Baton Rouge: Louisiana State University Press, 1991).

4. Warren, *All the King's Men*, 6.

5. Ibid., 8–11; see Proverbs 27:20, "Sheol and Abaddon [realms where the dead go, death itself] are never satisfied, and never satisfied are the eyes of man" (Revised Standard Version).

6. Frank P. Fury, "Sports, Politics, and the Corruption of Power in Robert Penn Warren's *All the King's Men*," *Aethlon* 22, no. 2 (Spring 2005): 68–69.

7. Sanford Pinsker, "Willie Stark and the Long, Thinning Shadow of Robert Penn Warren's *All the King's Men*," *Virginia Quarterly Review*, Fall 2004, 222.

8. Warren, *All the King's Men*, 26.

9. Ibid., 26–27.

## 8. The Pandering Populist

1. Tom Eblen, email to the author, May 31, 2017.
2. Warren, *All the King's Men,* 72.
3. Washburn, "At 70, *All the King's Men.*"
4. Warren, *All the King's Men,* 90.
5. Ibid., 91.
6. Washburn, "At 70, *All the King's Men.*"
7. Harold Woodell, "From Huey Long to Willie Stark: Louisiana Politics in *All the King's Men,*" in *Songs of the New South: Writing Contemporary Louisiana,* ed. Suzanne Disheroon Green and Lisa Abney (Westport, CT: Greenwood Press, 2001), 70.
8. Oates, *"All the King's Men*—a Case of Misreading?"
9. Steven D. Ealy, "Willie Stark as Political Leader," *Perspectives on Political Science* 37, no. 2 (Spring 2008): 92.
10. Warren, *All the King's Men,* 145–46.
11. Ibid., 146, 152.
12. Oates, *"All the King's Men*—a Case of Misreading?"; Warren, *All the King's Men* (play), act 3, p. 225.
13. Block and Elving, "Willie Stark Lives On."
14. Woodell, "From Huey Long to Willie Stark," 71–72.

## 9. The King's Man

1. Robert Penn Warren, *Proud Flesh,* in *Robert Penn Warren's* All the King's Men, ed. Grimshaw and Perkins, 19–100; O'Connor and Warren, "Interview with Flannery O'Connor and Robert Penn Warren," 26. For one instance where Warren talks about how he arrived at the Burden character, see his introduction to the Italian translation of the play, quoted in Grimshaw and Perkins, "Introduction," 9.
2. O'Connor and Warren, "Interview with Flannery O'Connor and Robert Penn Warren," 26.
3. Warren, *All the King's Men,* 63.
4. Ibid., 70.
5. Ibid., 98.
6. Ibid., 107–8.
7. Norton R. Girault, "The Narrator's Mind as Symbol: An Analysis of *All the King's Men,*" *Accent* 7 (1947), reprinted in *Robert Penn Warren,* ed. Nakadate, 61; Thomas Daniel Young, *The Past in the Present: A Thematic Study of Modern Southern Fiction* (Baton Rouge: Louisiana State University Press, 1981), 68; Robert B. Heilman, "Melpomene as Wallflower; or, The Reading of Tragedy," *Sewanee Review* 55 (1947), reprinted in *Robert Penn Warren: A Collection of Critical Essays,* ed. John Lewis Longley (New York: New York University Press, 1965), 83.
8. James Justus, *The Achievement of Robert Penn Warren* (Baton Rouge: Loui-

siana State University Press, 1981), 194–95; Leonard Casper, *Robert Penn Warren: The Dark and Bloody Ground* (Seattle: University of Washington Press, 1960), 122.

9. Warren, *All the King's Men* (play), prologue, p. 179, and act 2, p. 196. The Professor cuts himself off, and his statement remains unfinished, leaving the rest to implication.

10. Warren, *All the King's Men,* 188.

11. Jonathan S. Cullick, *Making History: The Biographical Narratives of Robert Penn Warren* (Baton Rouge: Louisiana State University Press, 2000), 117–18.

12. Ibid., 109, 115.

13. Warren, *All the King's Men,* 178, 188–89.

14. L. Hugh Moore, *Robert Penn Warren and History: "The Big Myth We Live"* (The Hague: Mouton, 1970), 16, 65, 70, 89. Moore articulates what I believe is the best description of the significance of history in *All the King's Men.*

15. Warren, *All the King's Men,* 438.

## 10. Putting Humpty Dumpty Back Together

1. Blotner, *Robert Penn Warren,* xiii, 236–37; Robert Penn Warren, "Blackberry Winter," in *The Circus in the Attic and Other Stories* (San Diego: Harcourt Brace, 1983), 84, 87.

2. Clark, *American Vision of Robert Penn Warren,* 100.

3. Warren, "Conversation," interview by Gado, 72–73.

4. Ibid., 75–76.

5. Ibid., 76.

6. Ibid., 78.

## Epilogue

1. Robert Penn Warren, "Evening Hawk," in *Collected Poems of Robert Penn Warren,* 326.

2. Robert Penn Warren, "Masts at Dawn," in *Collected Poems of Robert Penn Warren,* 233.

# Bibliography

## Works by Robert Penn Warren

Warren, Robert Penn. *All the King's Men.* New York: Harcourt Brace, 1946.

———. *All the King's Men* (play). Reprinted in *Robert Penn Warren's* All the King's Men: *Three Stage Versions,* edited by James A. Grimshaw Jr. and James A. Perkins, 173–227. Athens: University of Georgia Press, 2000.

———. *All the King's Men* (script). New York: Samuel French, n.d. At http://www.samuelfrench.com/p/12949/all-the-kings-men-warren. Accessed August 11, 2017.

———. *All the King's Men: The Matrix of Experience.* New Haven, CT: Yale University Press, 1963.

———. "*All the King's Men:* The Matrix of Experience." *Yale Review* 53 (1963): 161–67.

———. *Audubon: A Vision.* In *The Collected Poems of Robert Penn Warren,* edited by John Burt, 251–67. Baton Rouge: Louisiana State University Press, 1998.

———. "Blackberry Winter." In *The Circus in the Attic and Other Stories,* 63–87. San Diego: Harcourt Brace, 1983.

———. *Brother to Dragons.* 1953. Reprint. Baton Rouge: Louisiana State University Press, 1979.

———. *The Collected Poems of Robert Penn Warren.* Edited by John Burt. Baton Rouge: Louisiana State University Press, 1998.

———. "A Conversation with Robert Penn Warren." Interview by Frank Gado, February 8, 1966. In *Talking with Robert Penn Warren,* edited by Floyd Watkins, John Hiers, and Mary Louise Weaks, 68–85. Athens: University of Georgia Press, 1990.

———. "A Conversation with Robert Penn Warren." Interview by Bill Moyers. WNET Television, April 4, 1976. In *Conversations with Robert Penn Warren,* edited by Gloria L. Cronin and Ben Siegel, 93–111. Jackson: University Press of Mississippi, 2005.

———. "Evening Hawk." In *The Collected Poems of Robert Penn Warren,* edited by John Burt, 326. Baton Rouge: Louisiana State University Press, 1998.

———. "An Interview with Robert Penn Warren." Interview by Peter Stitt. In *Conversations with Robert Penn Warren,* edited by Gloria L. Cronin and Ben Siegel, 112–26. Jackson: University Press of Mississippi, 2005.

———. "Introduction to the Modern Library Edition." In *A Robert Penn Warren Reader,* 224–28. New York: Vintage Books, 1987.

———. "Masts at Dawn." In *The Collected Poems of Robert Penn Warren,* edited by John Burt, 233. Baton Rouge: Louisiana State University Press, 1998.

———. "A Note to *All the King's Men.*" *Sewanee Review* 61 (1953): 476–80.

———. *Portrait of a Father.* Lexington: University Press of Kentucky, 1988.

———. *Proud Flesh.* In *Robert Penn Warren's* All the King's Men: *Three Stage Versions,* edited by James A. Grimshaw Jr. and James A. Perkins, 19–100. Athens: University of Georgia Press, 2000.

———. "Robert Penn Warren: Willie Stark, Politics, and the Novel." Interview by William Kennedy, 1973. In *Conversations with Robert Penn Warren,* edited by Gloria L. Cronin and Ben Siegel, 84–92. Jackson: University Press of Mississippi, 2005.

———. *Robert Penn Warren's* All the King's Men: *Three Stage Versions.* Edited by James A. Grimshaw Jr. and James A. Perkins. Athens: University of Georgia Press, 2000.

———. *Selected Letters of Robert Penn Warren.* Vol. 1: *The Apprentice Years, 1924–1934.* Edited with an introduction by William Bedford Clark. Baton Rouge: Louisiana State University Press, 2000.

———. *Selected Letters of Robert Penn Warren.* Vol. 3: *Triumph and Transition, 1943–1952.* Edited by Randy Hendricks and James A. Perkins. Baton Rouge: Louisiana State University Press, 2006.

———. *Selected Letters of Robert Penn Warren.* Vol. 4: *New Beginnings and New Directions, 1953–1968.* Edited by Randy Hendricks and James A. Perkins. Baton Rouge: Louisiana State University Press, 2008.

———. *Selected Letters of Robert Penn Warren.* Vol. 6: *Toward Sunset, at a Great Height, 1980–1989.* Edited by Randy Hendricks and James A. Perkins. Baton Rouge: Louisiana State University Press, 2013.

———. "The World of Daniel Boone." *Holiday,* December 1963.

O'Connor, Flannery, and Robert Penn Warren. "An Interview with Flannery O'Connor and Robert Penn Warren." In *Conversations with Robert Penn Warren,* edited by Gloria L. Cronin and Ben Siegel, 23–36. Jackson: University Press of Mississippi, 2005.

## Films and Screenplays

Burns, Ken. *Huey Long.* PBS documentary, aired September 28, 1985. At http://www.pbs.org/kenburns/hueylong/.

Floyd, Carlisle, score and libretto. *Willie Stark, the Opera.* Staging by Harold Prince. Houston Grand Opera, PBS, 1981. At https://vimeo.com/134655406.

Nichols, Mike, dir. *Primary Colors.* Screenplay by Elaine May. Universal Studios, 1998.

Pakula, Alan J., dir. *All the President's Men*. Screenplay by William Goldman. Warner Brothers, 1976.

Rossen, Robert, dir. *All the King's Men*. Screenplay by Robert Rossen. Columbia Pictures, 1949.

Zaillian, Steven, dir. *All the King's Men*. Screenplay by Steven Zaillian. Columbia Pictures, 2006.

## Unpublished Interviews and Personal Communications

Benson, Michael. Email to the author, June 6, 2017.

Beshear, Steve. Email to the author, April 26, 2017.

Combs, Sara. Email to the author, May 12, 2017.

Cross, Al. Email to the author, June 3, 2017.

Cunningham, Bill. Email to the author, April 13, 2017.

Eblen, Tom. Email to the author, May 31, 2017.

Goodman, Bill. Email to the author, May 29, 2017.

Hawpe, David. Email to the author, May 24, 2017.

Lucke, Jamie. Email to the author, May 31, 2017.

Mearns, Geoffrey. Interview by the author, Highland Heights, KY, April 14, 2017.

Neikirk, Mark. Email to the author, April 19, 2017.

Ransdell, Gary. Email to the author, May 1, 2017.

Thompson, Aaron. Email to the author, May 15, 2017.

## Articles and Books

"100 Best Novels." Modern Library, n.d. At http://www.modernlibrary.com/top-100/100-best-novels/.

Anonymous [Klein, Joe]. *Primary Colors: A Novel of Politics*. New York: Random House, 1996.

"Author Robert Penn Warren Honored on U.S. Postage Stamp." PR Newswire, April 4, 2005. At http://www.prnewswire.com/news-releases/author-robert-penn-warren-honored-on-us-postage-stamp-54169642.html.

Basso, Hamilton. "The Huey Long Legend." *Life*, December 9, 1946.

Bernstein, Carl, and Bob Woodward. *All the President's Men*. New York: Simon and Schuster, 1974.

Block, Melissa, host, and Ron Elving. "Willie Stark Lives On." *All Things Considered*, National Public Radio, September 8, 2008. At http://www.npr.org/templates/story/story.php?storyId=94394578.

Blotner, Joseph. *Robert Penn Warren: A Biography*. New York: Random House, 1997.

Boosey & Hawkes. "Floyd, Carlisle: *Willie Stark* (1980)." N.d. At http://www.boosey.com/pages/opera/moredetails?musicid=6995. Accessed August 11, 2017.

"Broader Consequences" (editorial). *Frankfort State Journal*, January 28, 2003.

Casper, Leonard. *Robert Penn Warren: The Dark and Bloody Ground.* Seattle: University of Washington Press, 1960.

Center for Robert Penn Warren Studies, Western Kentucky University. Website, n.d. At https://www.wku.edu/rpw/. Accessed August 11, 2017.

Clark, William Bedford. *The American Vision of Robert Penn Warren.* Lexington: University Press of Kentucky, 1991.

———. "From *All the King's Men* to *Primary Colors.*" *America,* December 28, 1996, 26–28.

Cronin, Gloria L., and Ben Siegel, eds. *Conversations with Robert Penn Warren.* Jackson: University Press of Mississippi, 2005.

Cullick, Jonathan S. *Making History: The Biographical Narratives of Robert Penn Warren.* Baton Rouge: Louisiana State University Press, 2000.

Duka, John. "*Willie Stark*: From Opera House to Home Screen." *New York Times,* September 27, 1981. At http://www.nytimescom/1981/09/27/theater/willie-stark-from-opera-house-to-home-screen.html?pagewanted=all.

Ealy, Steven D. "Willie Stark as Political Leader." *Perspectives on Political Science* 37, no. 2 (Spring 2008): 91–97.

Eskew, Carter. "Is Obama Supporting Clinton or Sanders?" *Washington Post,* January 29, 2016.

Ferris, Lucy. *Sleeping with the Boss: Female Subjectivity and Narrative Pattern in Robert Penn Warren.* Baton Rouge: Louisiana State University Press, 1991.

Freedland, Jonathan. "Enough of Playing Hamlet: Obama Needs to Act Now." *Guardian,* September 3, 2013. At https://www.theguardian.com/commentisfree/2013/sep/03/enough-hamlet-obama-act-now-syria.

Fury, Frank P. "Sports, Politics, and the Corruption of Power in Robert Penn Warren's *All the King's Men.*" *Aethlon* 22, no. 2 (Spring 2005): 67–73.

Garner, Dwight. "70 Years On, It's Politics as Unusual." *New York Times,* April 12, 2016. At https://www.nytimes.com/2016/04/12/books/all-the-kings-men-now70-has-a-touch-of-2016.html.

Girault, Norton R. "The Narrator's Mind as Symbol: An Analysis of *All the King's Men.*" *Accent* 7 (1947). Reprinted in *Robert Penn Warren: Critical Perspectives,* edited by Neil Nakadate, 60–76. Lexington: University Press of Kentucky, 1981.

Goldberg, Jonah. "Trump and Sanders Break the Mold for Populist Politicians." *National Review,* December 30, 2015. At http://www.nationalreview.com/article/429087/donald-trump-bernie-sanderss-populist-politics?target=author&tid=897.

Gottschall, Jonathan. *The Storytelling Animal: How Stories Make Us Human.* Boston: Mariner Books, 2013.

Grimshaw, James A., Jr., and James A. Perkins. "Introduction." In *Robert Penn Warren's* All the King's Men: *Three Stage Versions,* edited by James A. Grimshaw Jr. and James A. Perkins, 1–18. Athens: University of Georgia Press, 2000.

Guthrie, Kentucky. "About." N.d. At http://guthrieky.com/about-2/. Accessed August 11, 2017.

Heilman, Robert B. "Melpomene as Wallflower; or, The Reading of Tragedy." *Sewanee Review* 55 (1947). Reprinted in *Robert Penn Warren: A Collection of Critical Essays,* edited by John Lewis Longley, 82–95. New York: New York University Press, 1965.

Henahan, Donal. "Floyd's *Willie.*" *New York Times,* April 27, 1981. At http://www.nytimes.com/1981/04/27/arts/opera-floyd-s-willie.html.

Justus, James. *The Achievement of Robert Penn Warren.* Baton Rouge: Louisiana State University Press, 1981.

Kentucky Arts Council. "Kentucky Writers' Day." N.d. At http://artscouncil.ky.gov/KAC/Showcasing/Event_WritersDay.htm. Accessed August 11, 2017.

Kentucky Historical Society. Historical Marker Database. N.d. At http://migration.kentucky.gov/kyhs/hmdb/MarkerSearch.aspx?mode=All. Accessed August 11, 2017.

Kirsch, Adam. "Willie Stark, the Un-Obama, and Idealism's Limits." *Toronto Star,* September 22, 2012.

Longley, John Lewis, ed. *Robert Penn Warren: A Collection of Critical Essays.* New York: New York University Press, 1965.

McCrum, Robert. "The 100 Best Novels: No. 67—*All the King's Men* by Robert Penn Warren (1946)." *Guardian,* December 29, 2014. At https://www.the-guardian.com/books/series/the-100-best-novels?page=2.

Moore, L. Hugh. *Robert Penn Warren and History: "The Big Myth We Live."* The Hague: Mouton, 1970.

Nakadate, Neil, ed. *Robert Penn Warren: Critical Perspectives.* Lexington: University Press of Kentucky, 1981.

Oates, Joyce Carol. *"All the King's Men*—a Case of Misreading?" Review of the restored edition of *All the King's Men* edited by Noel Polk. *New York Review of Books,* March 28, 2002. At http://www.nybooks.com/articles/2002/03/28/all-the-kings-mena-case-of-misreading/.

O'Connor, John J. "Carlisle Floyd's *Willie Stark* on PBS." *New York Times,* September 28, 1981. At http://www.nytimes.com/1981/09/28/arts/tv-carlisle-floyd-s-willie-stark-on-pbs.html.

Payne, Ladell. "Willie Stark and Huey Long: Atmosphere, Myth, or Suggestion?" *American Quarterly* 20 (1968): 580–95. Reprinted in *Robert Penn Warren: Critical Perspectives,* edited by Neil Nakadate, 77–92. Lexington: University Press of Kentucky, 1981.

Pinsker, Sanford. "Willie Stark and the Long, Thinning Shadow of Robert Penn Warren's *All the King's Men.*" *Virginia Quarterly Review,* Fall 2004, 222–32.

Robert Penn Warren Birthplace Museum. Website, n.d. At https://www.robertpennwarren.com/birthpla.html. Accessed August 11, 2017.

Robert Penn Warren Center and Library, Western Kentucky University. Website, n.d. At https://www.wku.edu/rpw/ and https://www.wku.edu/library/dlsc/kentucky-library/rpwlib.php. Accessed August 11, 2017.

Robert Penn Warren Circle. Website, n.d. At http://www.robertpennwarren.com/. Accessed August 11, 2017.

Seligman, Martin E. P., and John Tierney. "We Aren't Built to Live in the Moment." *New York Times,* May 19, 2017. At https://www.nytimes.com/2017/05/19/opinion/sunday/why-the-future-is-always-on-your-mind.html?_r=0.

Smith, Mark Caleb. "All of Trump's Men: This Race Is Starting to Remind Us of a Novel." *Dayton Daily News,* April 2, 2016. At http://www.mydaytondailynews.com/news/opinion/all-trump-men-this-race-starting-remind-novel/OwccmGIhxsRzRG47PQ1FbO/

Sweeny, Chuck. "Defiant Blagojevich Proves That Power Is the Ultimate Drug." *Rockford Register Star,* December 28, 2008. At http://www.rrstar.com/article/20081228/News/312289960.

Teachout, Terry. "The Prescience of a Political Novel." *Wall Street Journal,* March 24, 2016.

Truman, Cheryl. "Governor Alone Is Cause for Federal Aid." *Lexington Herald-Leader,* June 20, 2003.

Vauthier, Simone. "The Case of the Vanishing Narratee: An Inquiry into *All the King's Men.*" *Southern Literary Journal* 6, no. 2 (Spring 1974): 42–69.

Washburn, Michael. "At 70, *All the King's Men* Is the Book for This Campaign Season." WFPL radio, November 7, 2016. At http://wfpl.org/all-kings-men-book-campaign-season-2016/.

Watkins, Floyd, John Hiers, and Mary Louise Weaks, eds. *Talking with Robert Penn Warren.* Athens: University of Georgia Press, 1990.

Wattenberg, Daniel. "The Lady Macbeth of Little Rock." *American Spectator,* November 20, 2015. At https://spectator.org/64729_lady-macbeth-little-rock/.

Woodell, Harold. All the King's Men: *The Search for a Usable Past.* Twayne Masterwork Studies no. 112. New York: Twayne, 1993.

———. "From Huey Long to Willie Stark: Louisiana Politics in *All the King's Men.*" In *Songs of the New South: Writing Contemporary Louisiana,* edited by Suzanne Disheroon Green and Lisa Abney, 67–73. Westport, CT: Greenwood Press, 2001.

Young, Thomas Daniel. *The Past in the Present: A Thematic Study of Modern Southern Fiction.* Baton Rouge: Louisiana State University Press, 1981.

# Index